# Higher Self

# Higher Self

## Reclaiming the Power of Your Intuition

### Mory Fontanez

**DEY**ST.
*An Imprint of* **WILLIAM MORROW**

MEET YOUR HIGHER SELF. Copyright © 2025 by Mory Fontanez. All rights reserved. Printed in the United States of America. No part of this book may be used or reproduced in any manner whatsoever without written permission except in the case of brief quotations embodied in critical articles and reviews. For information, address HarperCollins Publishers, 195 Broadway, New York, NY 10007.

HarperCollins books may be purchased for educational, business, or sales promotional use. For information, please email the Special Markets Department at SPsales@harpercollins.com.

FIRST EDITION

*Designed by Patrick Barry*

Library of Congress Cataloging-in-Publication Data has been applied for.
ISBN 978-0-06-330999-9

24 25 26 27 28 LBC 5 4 3 2 1

For Rhea, who held up the mirror,

And for my mother, who nurtured everything I see reflected there

# Contents

*Foreword by Alok Vaid-Menon* ........ 000
*Introduction* ........ 000

**PART I: BECOMING DISCONNECTED** ........ 000

   1: You Are Divine ........ 000
   2: The Sacrifice ........ 000
   3: Incepting Limiting Beliefs ........ 000
   4: My Teenage Hero ........ 000

**PART II: THE CRISIS OF DISCONNECTION** ........ 000

   5: The World Around You ........ 000
   6: Anything for Love ........ 000
   7: Hitting the Wall ........ 000
   8: Confusing a Job with Our Purpose ........ 000

**PART III: BECOMING RECONNECTED** ........ 000

   9: Making Room ........ 000
  10: Learning the Language of Your Soul ........ 000
  11: Trust and Faith ........ 000
  12: Embodying Your Higher Self ........ 000
  13: Changing Frequencies Means Changing Relationships ........ 000
  14: Emanating Love ........ 000

*Acknowledgments* ........ 000
*Notes* ........ 000

# Foreword

ALOK VAID-MENON

If I were a tour guide for this planet I would say that you absolutely must engage a coaching session with Mory Fontanez before leaving. There's nothing quite like it: the eighth marvel of the Earth. But I'm not. I'm a poet, which means I'll say that Mory is a publicist for the soul. In a society that continually peddles latent dissociation as personality, Mory was brought here to remind us all what really matters—why we got here in the first place and what makes life worth living. In a world that can feel so flat and aimless, Mory makes living tantalizing again. A creative act. She paints murals of possibility everywhere she goes. I've seen her bring the incandescence of a dance floor to a boardroom. I've seen her make CEOs break down in tears. I've seen her, firsthand, turn this self-hating playground of organs into a proud, self-loving artist. How ironic that in my foreword I get the pleasure of speaking to how Mory propels us forward. Beyond limiting belief systems, validation addiction, self-doubt. Beyond who we thought we were and toward who we were meant to be all along.

I've always believed that we become our best selves through one another. That's the paradox of self-actualization—it's communal. At a fundamental level, we need each other to get free. How silly: we are all out here looking for answers when what we needed all along was the right question. Mory has the right questions. Who taught us that we couldn't access the lives we always dreamed of? Who made us believe that living a good life requires trade-offs?

# Foreword

How have we come to mistake our trauma coping strategies as our personalities? I first met Mory at a dinner several years back and she turned to me and asked some iteration of, "Who are you outside of what you've been told you should be?" I haven't been the same ever since.

Before we met I felt stuck in between what was and what could be. Because my body lived in fear, my heart took refuge in *could*. I knew that there was so much I *could* do in my life, but . . . *But* was my comfortable place, both my mailing and my residential address. I outsourced my power to everything around me and refused to see what I was capable of myself. I was the embodiment of excuse, Mory the personification of transformation. It was a fatal encounter. In speaking to her I rediscovered a native language I thought I had lost as a child: hope.

Mory's teachings are not for the faint of heart. They are volatile. Precisely because they are so bejeweled with hope. We are accustomed to misery, the monotonous drone of obligation, not elation. It's easier to stay in the realm of the familiar—even when what's familiar is pain. Hope hurts because it makes us discard the armor of cynicism. Exposes us to a sun inside ourselves we dimmed because we were taught that love is a disappearing act, not a show-and-tell.

There are so many gifts Mory has bestowed upon me through the years but hope is the most precious. With all of the diffuse despair and destruction around us I often find myself losing hope. Then, I immerse myself in Mory's quiet genius and she reignites my imagination, insists that there are feelings we haven't felt yet, words we haven't articulated yet, worlds we haven't built yet. When she speaks it makes the world make sense again: with the precision and bravado of a chiropractor, Mory performs her adjustment and you're back up and moving. She has left a permanent fingerprint on my heart. And I truly believe this book will do the same for you. She has helped me come back to myself after so long. How lucky it feels to be here. I guess this is my way of saying: welcome home.

# Higher Self

# Introduction

**W**e are, *in our* truest form, full of dignity, clarity, and a deep knowing. Made of an ancient thread, this knowing has pulled your soul throughout time and space to this place at this moment. It has been your constant, unwavering guide. Even if you don't always remember it's there.

And the thing is, most of us have forgotten who we are.

You see, most of the time, instead of remembering this profound truth of your identity, *fear* has defined and dominated your reality. Filling you with *can'ts* and *shouldn'ts*, fear is working hard to keep you small. From this contracted space, your capabilities and possibilities become incredibly limited.

Fear does this, not from a spiteful place but from one important intention: to keep you safe. From the moment you became aware of it, fear has been working hard to protect you from pain and suffering. It believes that keeping you small and living in a limited belief system about who you are and what you're capable of will keep all heartbreak at bay.

The problem is, despite its intention, fear keeps you trapped in the very space of pain and suffering it is working so hard to protect you from. Staying small to remain safe is the most painful place to find yourself. That's why you're here now. Some part of you is ready to unravel from the tight ball you've kept yourself in, to spread your glorious limbs, to stand tall and to exist in the full majesty of your largest, most empowered self.

Welcome.

This book is your road map back to yourself. You'll learn how to understand how your fear self was shaped, what it's working so hard to protect you from, and how to work with this ferocious protector to find and reunite with your Higher Self, which is the truest, most powerful version of yourself. The purpose of this book is to help you integrate all parts of yourself into one holistic system that works together to propel you toward your greatest desires. In reading this book, you will learn how to unlock the most powerful and intuitive part of you while healing the parts that are afraid and have been holding you back. Within these pages is an invitation and a detailed map toward unlocking that Higher Self within.

*Who is this Higher Self?* you may be asking yourself. This book is meant to answer that question too. For now, I will say this: Your Higher Self is your soul's guide. It is the deepest and truest part of you, the one that that directs, empowers, and enlightens your life's journey. It is the calmest, most secure part of your spirit. It is the voice that whispers in your ear, pulling you closer to your dreams. It is your lighthouse, the pull that has always inexplicably moved you through your darkest, most terrifying storms toward the most empowered, truest version of you. It is you if you were free to be all that you are without abandon or condition.

Higher Self speaks to you through its own unique language—your intuition. You can hear this knowing guidance most clearly when you are unencumbered by doubt, fear, or limitation. The work, of course, is dialing back on the other signals in order to help your intuition shine through. Your Higher Self whispers to you through your intuition with one purpose: to reawaken you to your unshakable, divine truth. The good news: it has called you to this book because you are ready to step into your power.

So here you are, and here I am—your unlikely guide. I have no awards, no Ivy League degrees, no doctorates. My life hasn't been a streak of constant wins that allow me to sit here as an authority telling you how to make your dreams come true. I'm the daughter of immigrants. The product of a single mother struggling to put food on the table and a shelter over my head. A solid B student with no clear ambition people could marvel at in my younger days.

I've been a divorcée, a single mother, a woman on the brink so many times I've lost count. Not a monk or a therapist or a guru suddenly having her moment of divine enlightenment. Just a person who carried the pain of my childhood into adulthood, wrapping myself in what I thought was the perfect package, trying to survive. It led me to a career as a corporate shill, buying into the *should*s and the *shouldn't*s of corporate America.

After nearly twenty years of counseling some of the world's largest brand on strategy and managing their reputations, I was well set up to be a chief executive at one of those illustrious corporations. I was on the fast track. Promoted ten times before my thirty-fifth birthday, sitting in rooms with some of the business world's most powerful leaders, influencing their decisions. I was set to become the realization of the American Dream my parents immigrated to this country for.

Until I couldn't take it anymore. I was miserable, overworked, and so far from my purpose. The pretty package started to unravel when my Higher Self began calling to me. With great force she challenged me to ask myself, *Am I really living my purpose? Am I using my gifts to help others to the greatest extent possible?* I couldn't ignore those questions. My Higher Self became insistent until I listened. She would break into meetings, distracting me from the topic at hand. She'd follow me home, reminding me that being busy was not the same as doing my purpose. She haunted me by reminding me constantly how small and unfulfilled I felt in the "successful" life I had constructed.

It was during this fight with my Higher Self that I realized something that changed my life. In all my travels, all my experience as a PR pro, a crisis manager, a maker of images, a counselor to powerful leaders and celebrities, I discovered that all of us have deep, effective, and 100 percent spot-on wisdom inside us. That wisdom always knows the answer and never steers us astray.

The problem is that we've been taught not to listen. Conditioned by a culture that tells us to value other people's opinions over our own, our inner wisdom has been vilified. I saw clearly how this dynamic works in favor of these systems of power: convincing us that our inner voice is wrong so that we abandon our truth and follow them like zombies.

And what happens then?

We learn to trust others more than ourselves, so we make decisions that are better for them than for us. We learn to ignore our own purpose so we can work harder for other people's dreams than we do our own. We learn to nod and agree, so others can be comfortable while we shrink. We forget the inner wisdom that would allow us not just to survive, but to *thrive*.

That is what my Higher Self was trying to get me to see all along. So, I took a hard left turn on the path of my life. I embraced my gifts of intuitive knowing and healing inner shadows. Instead of becoming one of those chief executives, I've built a thriving practice that reintroduces people to their Higher Self. By finally embracing my most innate gifts and my purpose, I find myself across the table from some of our cultures' most recognizable faces, guiding them lovingly toward healing their pain, breaking free of their limitations, and ultimately stepping into their Higher Self. While I can't name all the names or tell you the stories of each one of these world changers, what I can do is bring this work directly to you. I can take my journey, the one that led me to the most complete sense of well-being I've ever known, and plot its twists and turns for you in such painstaking detail that if you choose, you can follow the same path toward self-acceptance, love, empowerment, and a consistent sense of fulfillment. It can be done. I've seen so many people break through the shackles of fear and shame, stepping into the expansiveness of their freest, most loving selves.

We are about to go on a profoundly transformative journey together. In this book, I will walk you through your own life journey to understand how you came into the world, what caused you to disconnect from your own inner wisdom and ultimately, I will guide you back to reconnect to your deep, ancient, powerful inner knowing, your Higher Self.

This book is my method, wrapped in stories and hard-earned life lessons from me and my clients. It is part coaching, part memoir, part case study. The point of this book isn't to tell you a chronological story about me, it's to help you understand yourself through important themes in your own life. And so, this book is organized in three parts to help you both do the work and reconnect to all parts of yourself:

> PART 1: Identifying your fear self and the origin of your limiting beliefs.
>
> PART 2: Helping heal your limiting beliefs to create space to hear your Higher Self.
>
> PART 3: Embodying your Higher Self by reconnecting to your intuitive wisdom.

You'll notice that the first part of the book is written as a story about you, and about me. That is purposeful. I want you to really go back there and see your early years from an entirely new perspective while I share my journey with you. This viewpoint will prepare you for some important information about the world in which you're operating, and give important context about your own journey. You might not have recognized certain things as being speed bumps in your quest for growth, but looking at it this way is critical to unlocking access to your Higher Self.

Then, in the second part of this book, we'll examine the systems that have convinced you to doubt your own truth. We'll explore the working world, our relationships with media, education, capitalism, and with each other, to understand how each of these individual spheres work together to further separate us from Higher Self. In doing this, we'll take their power away, clearing the path even further for our reunion to our profound inner wisdom.

And finally, we will land, back to a place of reconnection to your Higher Self. In the third part of this book, I will show you exactly how to find and stay connected to this mighty part of you. I want you to leave this journey with total clarity and practical, real-life guidance about how to easily tap this wisdom and use it to create a life of total presence, fulfillment and, most important, a life that allows you to stand tall in the dignity of who you truly are.

Are you ready to rekindle that fire? Are you ready to return to your Higher Self?

Let's get started.

PART I

# Becoming Disconnected

CHAPTER 1

# You Are Divine

You were born completely whole. There was nothing lacking, nothing not good enough, nothing you needed to strive for. By simply existing, you were perfect.

Even better, you came into the world completely open. You had absolutely no ideas formed about who you are, no judgments about the people present in your life, and no demands on your environment. You existed simply to explore and understand yourself and the world around you.

In those very early days, you were focused on simple things: where your food was coming from and how comfortable or uncomfortable your environment was. You experienced those comforts or discomforts as they came, with no stories attached as to why they were happening to you. If your mom was an hour late to nurse you, you felt the hunger pangs and you cried out in discomfort, but you didn't draw any conclusions. There was no: "Maybe my needs don't matter," or "Maybe she doesn't care enough," or "Maybe I'm not lovable enough." You had no judgment. As soon as you were fed, you moved on from your discomfort, completely content to take in the next moment.

From the outside looking in, your parents probably saw you as small and defenseless, your eyes searching to understand, your face scrunched up at the sensation of something new. From their perspective, that was all there was to you: a newborn baby in need of their care.

But you knew better.

On the inside, you were privy to a rich world. One where there wasn't just you, a newborn baby with only a connection to your parents. On the inside, there was a whole expanse of energy that made up the essence of you. A knowing and powerful aspect that was far wiser an entity than what your parents could see on the outside: your soul.

Here's maybe where I should tell you what a *soul* is, from my perspective:

When we are born, we manifest into a physical form on this planet as a function of our soul. Our soul is our *intangible* form wanting to experience life, which is a *tangible* experience. Our soul is perpetually in search of tangible experiences so that it can learn and continue to expand from those lessons and experiences. Our souls only desire expansion. The only way for our souls to get those experiences is through a tangible form, our bodies.

Your body is the home your soul inhabits so it can have the tangible experiences it needs in order to grow. But when you land here, you forget, through a lot of conditioning, what your soul wanted to manifest, make tangible so that it could experience, in the first place.

This is where your **intuition** comes in. *Intuition* is defined by the Oxford English Dictionary as "the ability to understand something immediately, without the need for conscious reasoning." Throughout the ages, philosophers like Plato, Descartes, Sri Aurobindo, and Carl Jung have contemplated intuition. While their definitions and applications vary, all tend to agree that intuition is a "pre-existing" knowledge and connected to "greater consciousness." Intuition is the knowing we have that we just can't explain.

In my view, intuition is your soul's GPS, always sending you directions that fulfill your soul's desires. Intuition whispers, guides, and pushes without being too frightening or overbearing simply by placing a knowing into you that you can't explain.

Okay, we took a quick detour, but now, let's get back to little you. You're pretty cute and you've been waiting so patiently to get your story told. Your parents look down at your sweet baby face and believe you are simply mush, giggles, and dirty diapers. But without them knowing, your littlest self and an older, wiser part of you are working quite well together. Your intuition would push you to experience without abandon—taste this, touch that, stare at the other. You without doubt or question would comply. This harmony between the part of you living out the experience and the part driving you toward those experiences existed effortlessly and without question.

During this time, taking in the world was your only job, and you used two methods to understand your new surroundings: tactilely and through energy. The tactile experience gave you a sense of what the new world looked and felt like in a very tangible way: the prickliness of Dad's beard as he holds you, the smell of Mom's skin as she nurses you, the soft fur of the dog who can't get enough of you.

The energetic experience was a little more nuanced but just as powerful. As an infant, without the ability to communicate through language, your senses were heightened. Studies show that infants become attuned to the emotions of those around them within their first year of life, a critical capability for their survival.[1] Back then, you were more easily able to sense the energy of the room, to pick up on the feelings of others.

At this stage in your life, this unspoken, energetic connection between you and your caregivers was important to your sense of the world. What's most magical, though, is that you experienced the energy of others *without forming any ideas about yourself based on what they were giving*. This is key. The energy you may have felt from your caregivers, whether that was stress, sadness, calm, happiness, anger, or worry, was simply information with no bearing on who you were.

This ability to take in these encounters without experiencing the energy attached to them as having to do with you is directly thanks to the much louder, inner dialogue happening inside you. Your intuition was forcefully saying, *Keep going, keep experiencing, you are perfect as you are.* Even though your intuition will continue to whisper this your entire life, infancy is the moment of greatest connection because the signal is clean, clear of any interference from the outside world. Your brand-new self has this quality of being openly curious, unencumbered by the feelings or ideas of another. Remember that this part of you is fully entwined with you as you begin to experience the world. As you grow out of early infanthood into learning to crawl and walk, you do exactly that with an abundance of enthusiasm and joy.

*Toddlerhood.* Now you can really move! Your ability to experience everything just exploded, and, man, are you ready to follow the voice of your Higher Self into more experiences as your physical and mental capabilities expand. Great! Right? Well, for you, yes, it's amazing, but unfortunately, this growth of yours can be met with a different energy from those around you.

As you begin to take in the world, you are filled with energy, joy, and new ideas. This makes you talkative, hyper, excitable, and that is sometimes very exhausting for adults. Even though you aren't aware of it at this stage, the adults around you are often conditioned to label this exuberance in negative ways. Does the term "terrible twos" sound familiar?

Right now, you're excited to get your little hands on everything. You're more curious and awed by the wonders all around you than ever. You go outside and are blown away by a tiny blade of grass and how a little ladybug can climb from that grass onto your fingertips. You look up at the sky and, in the clouds, you see an entire world that engrosses you completely. Everything else fades away.

Your imagination is bursting into Technicolor during this time. There aren't any real boundaries between the physical world and what you're able to dream up. Birds could swoop down and fly you way up into those fluffy clouds. It's all so exciting that you have to share this experience! Your little self is wondering, *Are you people seeing this?!*

So, you begin to share this fantastical world with those around you. As you find words, you excitedly spew all that you're seeing and feeling. You look up at the person you've just let into your world ready and excited for them to join you, to encourage you to continue this wide-eyed creation of your world.

When I first met my stepson, the youngest of the four in our blended family, he was three. One weekend, we went to visit my in-laws in Lake Tahoe, and I watched as he climbed over the rocks in the nearby creek, looked around seriously, zeroed in on a spot, and hunkered down on a big rock in the middle of the running water. An hour later, I came back to the window to find him still there, completely engrossed. I could see his little lips moving excitedly, his hands outstretched at something I couldn't see. There was definitely something going on in that creek, and I needed to know what it was.

I walked outside, climbed over those rocks, and sat next to him.

"What's happening out here, Quinn?"

He looked up at me, eyes wide with some mix of joy and terror, and whispered his secret: the people in the tiny Village of the Rock needed his help—a monster was after them. I was there just in time. Could I help him build the fort these tiny rock people so desperately needed? Would I help him protect them?

Who could turn down such an important mission? Not me.

I got to work immediately, and in doing so, I completely abandoned my own reality so that I could take him up on his offer to enter his.

We worked hard that morning. We built a rock fort so solid no monster could ever break through, and as we worked, I asked him every question I could think of about this tiny world. As he described intricate details of the world, I could see his little self and his great big soul engaged in limitless creation. His eyes widened with every question, his enthusiasm grew, he opened up more, shared even more of what was happening inside with me. This was his reaction to being fully witnessed as his truest self.

Who was that person who met your wonder and curiosity with

their own? Was there one particular person you can think of—a parent, teacher, or sibling—who celebrated your joy? Or if you didn't have someone available in your immediate orbit, did you form a sort of parasocial relationship with a public figure—an actor, singer, athlete, and so on—whose gifts mirrored your own?

We'll call this person the cheerleader. At first, they are here to greet your wonder with their own, to encourage your soul's awe-filled curiosity in whatever direction it meanders. However, soon that curiosity will be attracted less toward a person and more toward specific things. A skill, like putting paint on paper (or the walls). Dance. Caretaking animals. Music. Soccer. Math. Cooking. Reading book after book. Your gifts begin to show up early. This person who was so important to you truly saw you or your gifts and made an effort to draw them out and support you on your path.

Maybe they commented on them or encouraged them. Maybe your mother saw how much you loved to read and signed you up for the summer reading program at the local library. Books became treasures, and new worlds opened to you. Maybe you were a performer, and you had an aunt or uncle tell you that you have a beautiful voice. Maybe they even invited you to sing in the car together. Whoever this person was, they nurtured your gift.

I have a client who is an artist. Their grandmother would paint with them—but not prescribe what needed to be on the canvas. This is an important distinction. When they were three, they distinctly remember that their grandmother would just give them a blank canvas and paint. Everything they made, their grandmother would spend time really examining the art. She took their work seriously, asking them about their composition and color choices. What an empowering conversation to have with a three-year-old! By her giving them credit for the genius they were showing as a tiny child, their gift was nurtured. That curiosity and creativity bursting forth from my client's young self found an outlet that allowed them to keep growing.

This is a key point of your development: At this stage, you're always striving to be seen. And if you're not seen, you still find a way. You're so fucking resilient that, even if you're not seen by the person around you, you find inspiration from heroes in books or on TV. As you look around to find confirmation that your desires and curiosities are worthy and shared, that feeling of being seen or reflected in others is a reminder that your intuition is there and being celebrated.

Back then, when your intuition was in charge, it began to dream without limits. This is one of the beauties of your toddler self. Your dreams were astronomically big—perhaps even comically so to the adults around you. Maybe you wanted to be an astronaut, or you wanted to be the next Whitney Houston, or you wanted to cure cancer and learn how to fly. Maybe you wanted to be president and play for the Dodgers, *at the same time.* That could seem completely possible to your tiny self, who has no qualms about taking up so much space. Do you remember that giddiness? That sense of possibility? You name a dream, and your intuition says, *Why not?* That's what intuition is: a powerful belief and the ability to chase your dreams without fear.

Think of a flower. When you see a flower growing out of the ground, it emanates beauty—colorful, delicate, and sweet-smelling. This is us when we are connected to source. When you pick that flower to bring it home and make it yours, immediately it begins to wilt. This is us being separated from source to join our families. If you take that flower home by carefully digging it up to plant it in a pot, lovingly water it every day, and put it in the sunlight, chances are it will continue to flourish. This is us when we come into families that take our care seriously.

But what happens if instead, you take the flower home, leave it out on the counter, and forget about it? Slowly it begins to shrivel, its beautiful, colorful petals turning brown, mold growing around the stem. The flower begins to decay. This is us when our care is completely ignored. But, as the flower continues to decompose, does its material change? Does it become something different, or is it, in its essence, still a flower? This is how love works. We are love, even when we are left to rot.

My hope is that you were surrounded by these cheerleaders that saw your truth and helped you continue to run toward it. What I know is that, unfortunately, and through no malicious intent, the adults around you at this critical moment were most likely trapped in a hurricane of their own stresses, worries, and pain. At times, this most likely made them unavailable and unable to see your soul expressing itself through you. When those adults met your fantastical world of expansion, they may have shut it down. Hard.

Let's say you are enamored by the way the birds are flying at the park and begin zooming around like a bird. *Smack*—you run right into Dad, who's exhausted from his soul-sucking job, or Mom, who is drained after a day of trying to do it all. You are busy being the best bird you can be, and all they want to do is go home. What might they do or say when you run headlong into them?

More than likely? "That's *enough!* It's time to go now."

*Boom.* Instead of a sense of wonder, suddenly you begin to feel something new—something darker, something far more limiting.

In that moment, you experience their reaction as being directly related to your actions. You are completely unaware that their inner world isn't filled with the same magic and wonder that inhabits you. You don't know yet that they have forgotten that magic, that they are disconnected from that wise, loving voice, their intuition. You assume that their stern impatience is full of just as much connection to their truth as your boisterous excitement and desire to express yourself freely. Therefore, you must have done something wrong to provoke their anger.

For the first time in your little life, you experience something new: *shame*. Reality comes crashing down.

That rejection doesn't always have to be outright either. Those adults who are pulled into their own world of fear or anxiety might reject your truth in more subtle ways. They may not pay attention to you, they may respond to your excitement with dismissiveness, sending you the message that your wondrous inner world doesn't matter. Or, guided by cynicism they've built over a lifetime of hurt, they'll want to bring you back down to "reality" to protect you.

They might tell you that what you're perceiving is not real and spend time explaining their reality to make sure you value intelligence over imagination. They might begin to assign value judgments to the way you spend time based on their handed-down beliefs about success or being good. For example, maybe instead of spending hours getting muddy and tracking a mess into the house, you should be sitting with a puzzle or doing something more intellectual, quieter, and more in line with their version of "good."

As you were transported back to those days of wonder, how did it feel to be abruptly thrown into a reminder about shame? Did it feel sudden? Did it feel unfair? Did you feel confused? If so, then you are reliving how little you felt when first coming into contact with this sort of rejection. The experience felt intense because the introduction of shame was the first disconnect from your Higher Self. You know those whispers from intuition? They were coming from somewhere far bigger this whole time; your Higher Self is actually the one that's been in dialogue with you from the moment you were born.

### Understanding Your Higher Self

Your Higher Self is the aspect of you that is connected to all of consciousness. It is your biggest, most expansive, universal self. It is the you that directs, empowers, and enlightens your soul's journey through lifetimes as it grows to understand itself and its connection to all that is.

Some people link this to religion, but however you view it, at its core this is the energy of pure, unwavering, and unconditional love. From that love, creation is possible. Creation of life, experience, and growth. We are all a part of this energy, this consciousness. It is in us; we are it, it is us. Which makes us, of course, unlimited in our potential.

Your Higher Self is your reminder. It is your truth. It is what you are. Enough. Powerful. Loving. Wise. Connected. This is you, at your truest essence. All that it wants, or that you want, is for your soul to experience its desires in the time it has here.

This quality of not being weighed down by the meaning of your experiences is another reason this part of you is called your Higher Self. It's not a judgment on the other pieces of you that develop over time, it just simply means it is you when you are vibrating at your highest, purest frequency.

Your Higher Self is like a balloon that is able to float freely; it does not allow experiences to create stories that weigh it down. It is focused fully on your soul's desire to experience the things that will allow you to express the fullness of you, or, in other words, your truth. Beyond experiencing, remember that your Higher Self has a very clear job: to guide you toward your soul's purpose, the reason your soul took the form of a body. It does this through a very specific language: your intuition. That whisper you were hearing all along, that was your Higher Self guiding you toward your expansion.

But you need love. So, as your sense of wonder and joy run up against the emotions and reactions of your caregivers, your soul's reason for becoming embodied begins to fade, and so does your ability to access openness and joy as directed by your Higher Self.

Whatever the cause, the shutdown has happened. Your sense of childlike wonder begins to fade. You begin to see that your world and the world of those you rely on for safety and love are quite different.

Now, instead of an invitation to expand, you are met with a choice: to keep the love and protection of the people you so desperately need by accepting their version of reality, *or* to remain engrossed in your inner world.

Not really a choice, is it?

You begin to see that you have to abandon this great interior world of beauty and exploration to walk toward the world of the adults around you, so that you can get what you need to survive.

With that, you disentangle your little fingers from the deep, wise, Higher Self, your truest self, because suddenly it is dangerous. Suddenly, this voice is making you choose things that the ones you need don't agree with.

You give that limitless part of you one last look, and then you turn and begin to walk toward a new world, a world defined almost completely without you in mind.

EXPLORATION: *Revisiting Your Childhood*

Take a moment to find a quiet space, and bring with you a favorite writing tool and something on which you can write.

Close your eyes and take three deep breaths. As you take your third deep breath, bring into your mind's eye a younger version of yourself, at three, four, or five years old. Observe what you're doing. Where are you? Who's around? What are you doing? How are you feeling in this moment? What do you want? Are you getting it? If not, how are you reacting? If so, how are you feeling?

Now ask yourself this question: *What is something that I remember feeling excited about at this age?* Just allow your mind's eye to play this out for you, almost like an old home movie.

After you've spent a few minutes there watching this inner home movie, take five minutes (or as long as you'd like) to write what that experience was. This exercise will be helpful as we work through the rest of the method, so hold on to this writing as we'll revisit it later.

CHAPTER 2

# The Sacrifice

*As you leave toddlerhood and* enter early childhood, you start to become aware of your need for the people around you. You begin to walk away from your inner world toward the world of adults. You believe, without fully being able to articulate it, that this world is constructed by people who are fully aligned with their truth. You accept their beliefs as your own by taking the signals they send you as evidence of your goodness and worthiness—or the reverse.

You don't know it, but you've already chosen by this point to sacrifice your full, uninhibited connection with Higher Self. Up until now, that sacrifice meant that you abandoned your sense of childlike wonder, no longer believing in magic. Now the stakes are even higher. You're about to give up the freedom that comes with not spending a second worrying what other people think about you. (My daughter's insistence on wearing her *Beauty and the Beast* Belle costume with iridescent purple cowboy boots and sunglasses to every event was my constant reminder of this.)

Now the evidence for why that sacrifice is essential begins to start pouring in. You are small, defenseless, and full of need. You know for the first time in your life how important other people are to your sense of safety.

You begin to look at other kids in your kindergarten classroom for cues about what you should like. You start to imitate Mom or Dad or Grandma, using their tone of voice when they're upset or excited. People even find that cute, smiling at you mimicking the adults around you, telling you that you're doing something worthy of their praise.

Maybe your parents decided a team sport or dance or music was the right path to help construct you into the best future version of yourself. You're not just playing anymore. Now most things you do have a *why* attached to them—learning to take direction, being tougher, growing smarter, being better, learning to win.

In your little mind, these adult *why*s become obvious truths. You're most likely not encouraged to check in with that inner voice. Instead, what you believe is that what the adults around you want for you is the only answer available.

If you don't follow what those adults want for you, there are consequences. You begin to believe you will lose their love. In this belief, Higher Self continues to step aside, making room for a second aspect to be nurtured within: fear.

## *Sacrificing Our Truth for Belonging and Dignity*

My son, Kian, is a powerful and gentle soul. He came into the world with a fervor to him that was hard for most people to understand. We call him AGT—"against the grain"—because his first response to any adult is to disagree with them. This is part of his purpose, to challenge systems and deconstruct them so they can be reconstructed from a place of clarity. He's always asking, "Why?" He doesn't just accept the status quo. "Because I said so" is absolutely not a response he can stomach.

While he has this fight within, he's also the most loving, gentle boy you could meet, which makes him uncomfortable around physical aggression. For his father, raised under very different circumstances and in neighborhoods where fighting meant life or death, teaching his kids self-defense through the martial arts was everything. He put both Kian, and his sister, Reina, in Brazilian jiujitsu at the ages of six and eight, respectively.

My daughter, who thrives on asserting herself, loved jiujitsu. She'd be ready in her *gi*—the uniform you wear when practicing martial arts—and standing at the door with a twinkle in her eye. Not Kian. Every Monday and Wednesday, just before his dad would show up to take him to class, Kian would start to feel sick. His eyes welled up with tears, and with his chin quivering, he'd beg me to save him from going.

After seeing the disappointment in his father's eyes, he'd sniff, wipe away his tears, and get in the car. I watched him at practice, as he'd look to his dad mid-spar: *Look at me!* and *Are you proud?"* Behind those searching eyes was a different question he was working out: *Why am I here?* Behind that question was fear that if he told his dad what he needed, he might lose his love in the process.

After suffering through classes for almost two years, Kian found the words to tell his dad how he felt. Full credit to his dad, he was able to put aside his own upbringing and really see his son, and give him what he was asking for. But this doesn't always happen, does it? Often, as kids of five or six years old, we just go along with the plan so we can show how good we are.

How many years did you end up in an activity you didn't even like as a child? How did that shape your identity? Was that aligned with who you were on the inside?

Losing the ability to hear your inner voice is not your fault. Actually, it is very much out of your control. This need for validation is a part of our emotional and psychological makeup as humans as reflected in Maslow's hierarchy of needs. Once we, as humans, feel that we are physiologically safe, that we are fed and sheltered, we move up the hierarchy to needing a sense of financial security. Just beyond that we have two needs that guide our young selves toward this shift of valuing validation above all else: **belonging** and **dignity (or self-esteem)**.

Our need to belong is primal. Our ancestors relied on this love and belonging to build tribes and to ensure the survival of the group. The need for belonging is so deeply linked to our sense of safety that it is no wonder we are willing to trade in our inner world to get this need met. Depending on who is on the other side of it, and what trauma, triggers, and fears they have or have not healed, we receive a load of new information about what we need to do to be accepted and ultimately belong among them. This is where we begin to incept the stories of other people.

If, for example, your family was an immigrant family like mine, the hardship and pain they endured in leaving their homes and building a life in a foreign place created a plethora of stories. These are stories about work ethic, education, gender roles, racial identity, "respectable" professions, loss, grief, and hundreds of other things. Your family believed that these experiences earned them the authority to hand down and enforce their stories to their children, families, or communities. They saw this as an act of love to help protect, or propel, their loved ones forward.

This was the case with my family. My mother, father, and older sister left Iran before the Iranian Revolution in 1979 and landed in the United States in search of a better life. Much to my parents' surprise, one year later, I showed up, and suddenly they had one extra mouth to feed.

My father worked eighteen hours a day, eventually becoming executive chef and food and beverage director for Keystone Resort, in Keystone, Colorado, where we lived, to help make ends meet; my mom worked as a seamstress for the resort that employed him. She spent most of her time tucked away in the back room of the resort's laundry building with a wooden desk and an old Singer sewing machine. My sister, who is almost ten years older than me, was busy trying to make friends, fit in, and, unbeknownst to me, escape the chaos of our little home. Which left me with . . . me.

But not really.

This point in my life is when my superpower, and my kryptonite, came clearly into focus. See, part of being in touch with your Higher Self is being aware of your imperceivable gifts—the way you can sense things or just know certain things without being told them. For me, this gift was and always has been the ability to become keenly aware of other people's feelings. *All* their feelings. The parts they show on the outside, and confusingly, when I was a child, the deeper, darker, more intimate feelings they try so hard to bury on the inside.

I sense feelings by feeling them as if they are my own. If I am happy and I walk into a room where someone is feeling stressed or sad, I will quite literally feel like I'm suddenly anxious or sad. It's taken me decades to learn how to separate my own emotions from others', and in doing that, my purpose as a coach has manifested. Identifying those deeply buried emotions, by feeling them when I'm sitting with a client, is part of what helps them reconnect with, and ultimately reintegrate, the lost parts of themselves.

Getting to that clarity has been a long, winding path, full of pain and confusion. It started at three or four, when I didn't know how to separate my feelings from those of the people I loved, the people who were there to take care of me. Instead, at that time, all I knew was that if someone was having difficult feelings, it was my job to make them feel better and to take care of them, even if it meant abandoning me.

In one of our first sessions, I usually ask my clients to locate the very first memory they have of their core wound. That memory is a honing device that allows us to pinpoint the exact moment we turned away from our Higher Self to build a strategy that would protect us from the pain our little minds couldn't understand. Mine is this:

I'm four and in the back seat of my mom's Chevy Caprice. My sister is sitting up front with my mom. Loud, joyful Persian music is blasting from the speakers, and my mom is singing along with a smile stamped on her face. We left our condo in Keystone when the sun was still up, but after two hours in the car, it's dark and we're somewhere in Denver. We're looking for something, or someone. The car slows down.

"There," my mom says, "that's her house."

My sister chuckles bitterly. "Look," she says, pointing to the street in front of this house.

I recognize my father's red and tan Bronco, parked there on the street in front of a tiny row house.

Cold clarity settles on my mom's face. "I see," she says.

She turns toward me in the back seat, and in a flash, the smile reappears. She blows me a kiss, but I feel like I can't breathe. Her sadness, her brokenness, are like missiles, entering me like shards of glass.

*Fix her*, the scared little voice from inside says, *fix her, or we won't survive.*

I made an unspoken agreement with my mom in that moment: I would mend her heart, no matter what it took.

I took my job seriously. So seriously that I made my father my enemy. At four and five, I made it my purpose to treat my father like he was garbage. I'd ignore him when he'd walk into a room or sprawl myself across my mom every time he'd try to touch her, even just to greet her after work.

Everyone else in the house tiptoed in terror around my father's big temper and disinterested interactions, but I decided to fight him. He'd buy me gifts; I'd leave them untouched in the corner of my room. He wanted to watch TV when I was watching Saturday morning cartoons; I'd rage into the greatest temper tantrum I could muster until he'd leave the room in a huff. He'd try to speak to my mom; I'd pick that exact moment to need her so desperately she had to choose me. I slept in between them, every night, right until he left.

You would think this strategic takedown of my father would have kept me busy enough, but no, I still had time to feel and attend to my mom's every emotional need. I never left her alone. If I sensed she needed to feel needed, I'd become needier. If she wanted a laugh, I'd allow myself to be silly. She needed to feel loved, no problem: I'd follow her around and shower her with so much affection people started calling me her "shadow." I loved that title. "Her shadow" meant she never had to be without me. I could keep her safe.

My intuitive gift, a part of my Higher Self, became a tool my fear hijacked to protect me. Maybe then if someone had been around to explain to me that feeling other people's feelings is indeed a superpower but not something I had to overextend myself to "fix" for them, I'd have seen myself as my powerful Higher Self more clearly and known that I was safe no matter what. But, because my need for safety took over, I instead made the trade-off.

The automatic response "I'm great!" when I'd ask my mom what was wrong taught me that what I was sensing in my deepest wisdom—her sadness and heartbreak—was flat-out wrong. That I was crazy. And yet, I sensed it nonetheless, and to release the pressure of those hard feelings inside, I decided to keep showing up for my mom.

Everyone has a great gift. Everyone has the origin story of their core wound that subverted that great gift. What was yours? Do you have any sense of that first moment?

I know it's painful to go back there, but what's waiting is the truth about who you are really and how you were forced to walk away from that self to survive. That first moment of disconnect with your intuitive, wise Higher Self is your invitation back to connecting with it.

### The Final Betrayal

That first moment is just the beginning. In the early, childhood years, those moments come in quick succession, building a strong case for separation from your Higher Self. You have the origin story of your core wound, but this is followed by the story of the final blow—the moment you decide once and for all to leave Higher Self behind.

When I wasn't busy following my mom around, I spent hours outside building obstacle courses on the mountainside or walking down the path through the woods to the lake, taking in the pines, the hummingbirds, the majestic peaks that followed me wherever

I went. In all of these activities I was constantly in conversation with the unseen.

Not understanding that I was engaging with Higher Self, I needed to see someone on the other side of this invisible dialogue. I think we all do this, and our parents need a label for it too, so they call it our imaginary friend. Mine was no taller than three feet, brown from head to toe, and wore a little hat. I called him Googool. (No joke. Nineteen eighty-five and I came up with what sounded like *Google* as the name for my imaginary friend!)

Googool and I had endless adventures. We would go outside into the forest and look for treasure. We would try to find prints of baby deer or bear cubs, or we would run through the meadow to see how much pollen we could collect on my corduroys. Best of all, we would sit for hours inside my family's three-bedroom condo and play with my dolls while having full conversations about how I was feeling, what I was seeing, or what I thought about the world unfolding around us.

Googool became a major presence in our home beyond even just me—so much so that when we would sit around the *sofreh* (in the Persian way of dining, you sit around a cloth, or *sofreh*, on the ground instead of at a table), I would ask my mom to set a place for Googool, which she always did.

As my relationship with Googool was growing, so was I, and so was my deep longing for a relationship with my much older sister. She was everything beautiful and cool, and I wanted her attention *so bad*. For me at six or seven, my sister's affection (let's be honest—I would have just settled for attention) was a signal that I mattered. Her validation was like a drug. I would let her dress me up in dresses and jewelry and do my makeup like a little doll when she was bored. I would sit there at her record player with her for hours, picking up the needle for her every time she wanted to pause the song and write down the lyrics. Whatever it took to bask in her glow, I was game.

My sister, on the other hand, was living a very different story. At fifteen and sixteen years old, she was navigating a world far too complicated and adult for her. My mother leaned on her more as a friend than a daughter. She would confide in my teenage sister about my father's infidelities, share their ever-present financial stresses in anxiety-inducing detail, and rely on my sister to fill the void of love and emotional support that her own family, thousands of miles away in Iran, used to give her.

My sister had a lot to navigate, and she separated herself from me to do that—which only made me want her attention more. That was okay for the moment. I was still connected to my inner world, the one that came to life through Googool, and that connection eased my longing for my sister's acceptance. Until, that is, the noise of my need to be validated from the outside became louder than the whispers from deep within.

I still remember the moment the desire for my sister's approval and my inner world collided. One night, as we sat down at the *sofreh* for dinner with Googool in his standard spot, my sister walked into the room, looked at the empty place setting next to me, rolled her eyes, and sat down. She didn't even have to say anything. One look, and everything changed.

Right then I made a choice to give up my best friend, to trade in the creation made up of all those sweet inner whispers to hopefully get her instead. I stood up, announced that my sister had sat on Googool (I was shady—or maybe smart—enough to blame her for this loss), and went up to my room.

I never saw Googool again.

My sister was carrying so many of the stories, and associated pain, of our parents, and the generations before them. You don't have to be from an immigrant family to receive stories from your elders. These stories exist at all levels within all families: impoverished or privileged; Black, brown, or white; PhD or GED. The experience of fear is the great equalizer. When left unexplored and unhealed, whatever experiences caused pain ultimately calcify into fear. With that fear, our elders create a shield and pass it on to the next generation, almost like a sacred gift of protection.

For some of my clients, these inherited ideas take the form of statements like: *You have to say yes to everything, or else the opportunities will fade away* or *Be available to anyone who needs you if you want them to think you're relevant* or *It's okay if it doesn't feel right, it's a necessary evil.*

These limiting beliefs were handed to them from their families to protect them. What we learn together in our sessions is that these beliefs are harming them, causing them to stretch outside their own needs, do things that don't feel right, and move away from their truth and purpose. (For these clients I prescribe a new mantra, "No is an abundant word." This is meant to replace incepted beliefs with one that gives them permission to seek their own truth and invite even more opportunity by creating space for it.)

In most families, the intention in handing down these stories is beautiful: it's meant to protect their offspring. However, these stories are handed down without much consideration for who is receiving them. The storyteller doesn't think about what new perspectives or gifts the listener might have that their elders don't or didn't.

This moment is actually an invitation for you to break the ritual of passing down fear as a form of wisdom. You don't mean harm when you are doing it, but the harm is there, nonetheless. That's how unconsciously we do it. We take the limitations that faced our ancestors and make them our own, or we come face-to-face with their limitations and make them about us.

In the next chapter we're going to dive deep into these limiting beliefs, and later in the book I'm going to show you how to heal them. Right now, I want to take you back to your own story, the moment you may have decided your inner world was something you had to sacrifice to get your needs met. It happened at a much earlier age than I bet you're even aware of, and that part of you deserves to finally be seen for the sacrifice it made.

## The Moment of Rupture: Meeting our Fear Voice

Finding the moment we walked away from Higher Self and our inner truth is key in healing the separation. However, just like my decision to use my intuitive gifts to care for my mom or my casual but life-altering dismissal of Googol, I had no idea what I was giving up when I took away his seat at the table.

When I am working with a client, never, ever does that client come to the first session and say to me, "I was separated from my Higher Self at [x] age. This is when I was taught to stop choosing myself."

What happens instead is that someone comes to me when they're dealing with a current dynamic holding them back that says one of two things: they're not enough or they're too much. Through my work, I have come to understand that all of us come from one of these two core wounds: **you're not enough** or **you're too much**.

Which of these statements do you most relate to? "I'm not enough" would resonate if you feel like nothing you ever did was good enough or that you were somehow not visible in your family unit. "I'm too much" would speak to you if you experienced people asking you to quiet down, be less expressive, want or need less or if people expressed envy toward you in subtle or overt ways. These are two sides of the coin that both say, *You don't hold value.* More specifically, *You don't hold value until you do a certain thing that makes me happy.*

It is in our bid for dignity and belonging with others that we sacrifice our truth. In my case, my sister did not intend to have the impact she did. Most of the time, this is true. That said, while I wish this handing down of fear was always done to you by others without their meaning harm, sometimes the intention of passing down these stories can be harmful. Sometimes, either consciously or subconsciously, our caregivers use these stories to control our behavior or to manipulate us into serving their needs.

One of my clients, a prominent academic and author, recently told me during a session that their only value was in making other people's lives easier.

"Why?" I questioned.

"Well, that's what makes people love me, honestly," they replied.

"Where did that start? Can you locate that feeling of only being valuable when you make others comfortable? How far back does it go?"

Immediately they replied, "Six years old."

They went on to tell me about how their mother demanded emotional support from her children by using the simple phrase "If you want me to be okay, you will . . ." and then she would make some demand.

Of course this six-year-old wanted their mom to be okay. In fact, they *needed* her to be okay. So, what choice did they have but to do the thing she was asking to ensure she would do her job of caring for them? There was no room for their truth in that equation.

Unhealed trauma creates **fear.** The most common response to fear is protection, and sometimes protection turns into deeply harmful behaviors or characteristics.

Take narcissism, for example. A narcissist is often born out of trauma; focusing on self becomes a survival mechanism in the face of chaos. What happens when that narcissist becomes a parent? How can someone who has built a strategy of survival by focusing solely on themselves begin to make their life about someone else? Often, they can't, and often their children are recruited into their survival strategy, as with my client.

Guess what? If you were raised by a narcissist, you are most likely a people pleaser. Why? Because you were taught that taking care of the narcissist's needs was your most important, or even *only*, value. Your esteem becomes built around what you can do to make others okay.

This is not about blame. Quite the contrary, this exploration and analysis are about holding compassion for those who implanted these limiting stories in you while seeing those stories as separate from who you are. But to do that, you need to become intimately familiar with fear, specifically, *your* version of fear.

Fear came rushing in as the *second voice* in your inner world around the time of early adolescence. Fear was fierce and powerful. Fear shoved aside anything standing in its way to make room for it to sprawl out and take up space. Fear grew in you slowly at first. Then, it grew quicker as you grew and more keenly observed how those you loved had become entranced by it.

What do I mean? During this time in your life, you watched your parents, siblings, and others choose this fear voice rather their own Higher Self, over and over. Every time you excitedly shared news about your day and felt them drift off into their own world, mulling over their worries, you saw this new entity take form.

Every time you watched them hold back their exuberance, choosing to be "adult" instead of throwing themselves into play with full abandon, you saw this voice take over.

Every time they told you that you were too much, too loud, asked too many questions, had too much energy, talked too much, wanted too much, you were hearing fear.

Every time you heard the words *too much* in any form you knew that this creature was beginning to take hold inside you as well.

One minute, it was just you and Higher Self expressing the fullness of your truth. The next, fear came in to say it was time to shut it down. You and Higher Self tried to work around it, ignoring it at first, but then fear would say, *Don't you want them to love you?*

Fear represented the outside world. It informed you what other people might feel toward you. It told you what you needed to do to gain their love. If there was anything within you that said the opposite, fear worked hard to villainize it. Fear believed that Higher Self was a danger to you. It believed the more you followed the calling of your soul, the further you would be from the safety and belonging you so desperately needed.

As you grew into your late adolescence, fear began to tell you that Higher Self was silly, childish, and not cool. For me this was feeling that I had to abandon my imagination if I wanted my sister's acceptance. For some of my clients in the entertainment industry, it attempted to stop them by telling them to *grow up, stop being so naive* when they reached for dreams that seemed unreachable to their families.

The work we're doing together in this book is going to help you identify what the fear voice is saying, and what it needs, as much as help you learn how to recognize your Higher Self and its language of intuition.

In my work with clients, the dynamic I see is that "I am not enough" or "I am too much" is always active within. That core wound is still the one in the driver's seat, making decisions on behalf of the adult. Every time we trace that wound back, it returns to this moment in time, the moment they decided to turn away from their magic because they believed someone needed or wanted them to. They had to hide who they really were. They had to pretend to like things they didn't like, pretend to have interests they didn't have. They had to speak louder, speak softly, or be more cordial.

Whatever it was, their perceived survival became about morphing away from Higher Self and their truth. This moment matters because this is the exact point during which we lose sight of who we are. In this moment we forget that we are our Higher Self, this divine aspect sent here to experience and expand. In this moment we decide that we are the fear, the limitations, *the can't*s and the *shouldn't*s being projected onto us. This moment right here is where we confuse ourselves for being fearful, limited beings, disconnected from ourselves and each other. This is the moment we forget that we are innately divine. So, this is the moment we need to go back to.

In my work with clients, this is the path we walk together. Our eye is on meeting and reconnecting to Higher Self, on making decisions that are aligned with dignity and a sense of empowerment.

Just know that in this stage of early childhood, around five to eight, you were beginning to build evidence that turning your back on Higher Self was the right thing to do. Abandoning your inner wisdom made you smart, savvy, palatable, and lovable. Fear created the perfect breeding ground for other people's ideas to hold more value than your own, which led to the ultimate severing of your relationship with your Higher Self. In this moment you began to believe that you *were* this fear. You've carried that belief with you until now, as you read these words.

When we started working together, Alok Vaid-Menon was a beautiful and deeply confronting expression of being a nonbinary person in this world. Through their poetry, Alok jolted people into facing the truth of what we do to one another when we separate ourselves and "other" those who we don't understand. In doing this work, they ask us to confront our own shame, bringing us face-to-face with the depths of our own grief.

Today, Alok is one of the most prolific thinkers, artists, poets, authors, performers, and comedians you will ever come across. They have truly expanded into the fullest expression of the human experience: grief, yes, but also joy and love. This transition from a well-known poet and activist to a performer selling out comedy tours around the world came as Alok began to see themselves fully in the abundance of all they are.

In order to get there, Alok did the inner work to realize that grief was only one aspect of their human experience and their purpose in the world. The larger purpose, the larger self? They learned through their work to reconnect to Higher Self, which was love. In this work I slowly started to watch Alok shift from grief to joy, from responding to hate with love.

If you look up Alok today, you will run into one of their most popular social media posts. It starts with an image of one of the many death threats they receive. These hateful, threatening missives usually include some attack on the way Alok looks, followed by some form of asking them to stop existing altogether. Below the image of these messages, you will find a love letter from Alok to the sender: "I see you hate yourself," it will say, "so instead, I will love you."

Love is the other side of fear. Alok has become our living reminder of this world-changing message by working through their youngest fear self to locate their most loving, Higher Self.

EXPLORATION: *Understanding the First Moment of Sacrifice*

It is time to get well acquainted with the fear voice so you can understand how it has taken hold and what you gave up along the way. We are going to do this together over the next few chapters. Remember Maslow's hierarchy of needs? Let's work together to understand what beliefs have been incepted in you about who you need to be to get two of those very basic needs met: belonging and dignity.

Divide a sheet of paper into two columns. At the top of one column write *Belonging*. At the top of the second column write *Dignity*. For each column, list all of the things you heard or sensed your caregivers wanted you to be or do to get that need met from them. This could be as simple as *be a good kid* or as specific as *get straight A's in all my classes*. Whatever comes to mind, write it down in that column in a list.

All I want you to do for now is identify what falls into those two categories. We will come back to these lists at the end of the next chapter to unlock the truth about each belief and help heal it so you can move forward without the weight of those old stories.

CHAPTER 3

# Incepting Limiting Beliefs

By the time you entered your late childhood and edged toward adolescence (think eight to twelve years old) you needed a belief system about yourself to make sense of painful moments and survival strategies.

Your later adolescence was when you made some intense decisions about who you were. *I am . . .* —at this age, whatever you put after those words defined you, and still may define you today. At eight, nine, and ten, you started to fill in the space after *I am* with notions about yourself that helped explain why your life leading up to that point felt the way it did and why people in your life treated you the way they did.

Everything was about you, so their treatment of you was evidence that in some ways you must not have been enough. You needed to understand why, so you created beliefs about who you were to make sense of it all.

Had Higher Self been as much a part of you as it had been just four of five years before this point, you would have heard its voice clearly saying, *Those things weren't about you, my love, that was just them coping with life, forgetting their own Higher Self.*

But mostly, you've parted ways with Higher Self by now, which means that to explain these experiences with others, these *I am* statements were followed by projections from this core wound: you were not enough; something was wrong with you. This may just have been the exact moment your fear voice became officially louder than any other internal voice.

Fear is constantly filling your head during these later adolescent years. You are 100 percent certain that every single thing you experience from others has to do with you. Unlike your much younger self, who notices the negative energy coming off caregivers and is unsure what it's connected to, in this stage, you are certain that you are the root cause. You let that convince you that whatever you authentically are is causing others to reject or hurt you.

Through this strategy, fear begins to fill you with beliefs. These beliefs are designed to mold you into the most pleasing package to make choosing you easy for other people. Prior to this, without this fear-inflicted identity, you were free to be so many things without it meaning anything about you. Now, the pressure is on. Who you are decides how you will be loved.

Your limiting beliefs are, and have been since this moment in your life, your explanation for why you're not enough, and who you need to become in order to be worthy of love.

Without knowing it, the adults around you told you in a million ways what they needed you to be. While you are assuming they are doing this in your best interest, what they are doing is demanding an identity that will take care of them. Or, they are living so far outside their own truth that they have created a world of limitations that you mistake for reality.

If your mom hid her true feelings when your dad was angry, she may have taught you that silence is safety. If you watched your dad take on a new persona around his boss, he may have taught you that authenticity is dangerous. If your parents celebrated your A's and threw away your paintings, they may have incepted the idea that intellect is more valuable than creativity. If disagreement was seen as disrespect in your household, you may have learned dissent is betrayal.

As you walk the tightrope of enacting limiting beliefs that are not true to who you are, the world around you and the people in it start to feel confusing. So, you grab on to those belief systems more tightly. It becomes your mission to live them out.

This stage is probably when you also experienced your first taste of rejection outside your core family unit. Maybe other kids said you couldn't play with them. Someone made fun of your clothes. The popular kids didn't invite you to the birthday party. We all have a story.

Big or small, whatever it was, this new rejection attacked your sense of belonging. Not having any other information but the limiting beliefs you've created to explain your core wound ("I am not enough"), you decide that these experiences are also evidence that your core wound is true. Your limiting beliefs, the explanations for why you're not enough, grow.

When you look for evidence that you're not enough or that you're too much for people, you will find it. Always.

You've been looking for that evidence since these very early days. Without knowing it, you've been on a quest to find, in every interaction, every word, every experience, proof that your core wound and your limiting beliefs are in fact true.

Using that lens, you've found a thousand pieces of evidence and further entrenched your limiting beliefs about yourself, because there's proof, so it must be true!

## Limiting Belief Systems

Most of the thoughts you have about yourself and about life were incepted into you from the outside. Very few of these ideas are your own, which means the ideas you have about yourself are weighed down by the past experiences, fears, and hopes of the people who implanted them in you. These thoughts that exist within you, the thoughts that tell you whether you can or you can't, whether you're worthy or not, are called **limiting belief systems**.

They are the system of beliefs that limit you from reaching your potential, and they are never innate. Instead, they reflect the original believer, a projection you have accepted as reality. Limiting beliefs are the wall between you and your Higher Self. They are the thoughts we readily accept as we push our own intuition away.

Here are some common limiting beliefs I hear from my clients every day:

*I don't have what it takes to start a business.*

*I can't have a happy marriage and a successful career—something's gotta give.*

*I need to be available to my children 24/7 or they will feel abandoned.*

*I need other people's opinions before I make a decision.*

*It has to be perfect, or it won't be worthwhile.*

*I have to be perfect, or I won't be worthwhile.*

*My desires are dangerous.*

*My truth is dangerous and will leave me unloved and alone.*

*A college degree is what makes me respectable.*

*The other shoe will drop . . . eventually.*

*Love hurts.*

*Money is evil.*

*Joy is frivolous.*

Do any of these sound familiar?

I could write pages more of these beliefs. They are endless, and they are always limiting. Everyone has limiting beliefs because they are a part of the human condition, and they even have a function. One thing I always want you to remember as you heal your limiting beliefs and connect to your power is that no part of you is disposable; every part is working hard to try and protect you, even the parts that create suffering. Limiting beliefs are no different.

They're working hard at attempting to protect you, and in doing that they want you to stay as small and hidden as possible.

This is important to remember. Healing is not linear, and there is no end point. Healing is also not about fixing yourself. You are not broken. Healing is about learning to understand each part of yourself. Once you understand each aspect, the scared and the courageous, the limited and the limitless, you can begin to integrate them all into your being. In this work, that means your limited self and your Higher Self must begin to coexist. I use the figure eight, or infinity sign, to describe this to my clients.

## The Figure Eight

The figure eight, or infinity symbol, can be found in many cultures and traditions dating back thousands of years. Generally, all these traditions agree that the infinity symbol is about bringing harmony to disparate parts. In my method, this symbol is the meeting of our two selves: the human/limited/triggered self and the divine/Higher Self.

Our human bodies, housing our big purposeful souls, are quite literally where the cosmos and the earth meet. This is another way to think of our fearful/limited selves and our Higher Self—the part of us that is human and the part that is divine. To exist with maximum ease and expand to our fullest potential we need to be in flow between these two aspects: our fearful/limited self and our Higher Self. We can only maintain this constant flow when we are aware of the existence of both parts.

That's what this book is here to do—remind you that your Higher Self is just as much a part of you as the limited self. Up until now, you may have believed that this limited voice was the only voice, and so naturally, you follow its every call. But being aware that we have these two parts allows us to take care of the self who experienced harm and created limited beliefs while also listening in to the wise guidance of our divine/soulful or Higher Self.

Where we get stuck in this process is when we allow the limiting beliefs (and accompanying feelings of shame and guilt) to

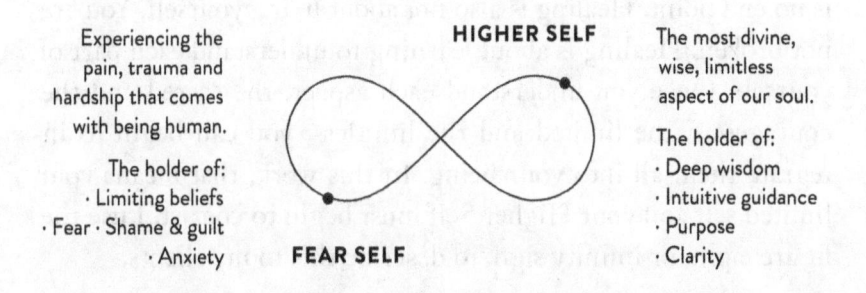

Experiencing the pain, trauma and hardship that comes with being human.

The holder of:
· Limiting beliefs
· Fear · Shame & guilt
· Anxiety

**HIGHER SELF**

**FEAR SELF**

The most divine, wise, limitless aspect of our soul.

The holder of:
· Deep wisdom
· Intuitive guidance
· Purpose
· Clarity

define our entire reality. This work is about the balance of the two things: the needs of the limited/fearful self and the guidance from the Higher Self.

A critical step in your journey to reconnect with Higher Self is identifying, diagnosing, and uprooting the limiting beliefs that have been incepted into you from a young age and are working so hard to keep you small. In this chapter, you will learn how limiting beliefs are handed down from generation to generation, as well as how to begin unraveling your system of limiting beliefs by finding their origins and using evidence to stamp them out.

Limiting beliefs are like non-native weeds: planted by someone other than you, quick to take over, but once pulled, they reveal the beauty of the garden beneath. One thing I always want you to remember as you heal your limiting beliefs and connect to your power is that no part of you is disposable. Every part is working hard to try and protect you, even the parts that create suffering.

### Generations of Limits

My grandmother on my mom's side was a pure ball of light. She even looked like a little ball: short, round face and tiny legs beneath a round body, always smiling, always telling you something profound behind her knowing eyes. We called her Aziz Joon, "dear one" in Farsi.

Aziz Joon was the closest thing I've ever come to divinity on this planet. When she prayed, magic would happen, whether it was my father returning to try and work things out with my mom after years of estrangement or a lost cell phone being returned by a kind cabbie. If Aziz Joon set her heart and her soul on something, she made it happen, every single time. She is the one who passed the gift of deep intuition to me. Part of me even thinks she knew I'd use it to heal others.

The most incredible thing about Aziz Joon was the way she moved with optimism and unconditional love despite having lived a brutal life. Born in a village eighty miles from Tehran in the late 1930s (we never knew her birthday because her family was too poor to get a birth certificate, or girls weren't considered valuable enough to have one—both are probably true), her mother died when she was just three years old. She was raised by a father who couldn't afford her, let alone understand her. To deal with this problem, her father married her to a widower and father of two, twenty-five years her senior, at the age of thirteen.

I remember my grandmother telling me stories about learning to make rice and instead making sludge, or her getting her first period and racing to clean herself off in the well they used to wash their dishes before her husband noticed, barely understanding what was happening to her body. She would laugh at herself while telling me these stories and continue laughing even when she'd describe her husband (my grandfather) getting impatient and, eventually, angry with her—resentful that she couldn't in fact take care of his home and his children as promised, as if a vow of marriage would have somehow turned this child into a wife overnight.

"But I learned fast!" she would say, beaming with pride. She'd tell me about all the ways she tried hard to master these tasks and how eventually he grew to love her, because she had done such a fine job of overcoming what she lacked.

*How can she be laughing!* I'd think. I was twelve years old and couldn't imagine what she'd been through. Even with that awareness that my grandmother had been robbed of her childhood, that her laughter was masking tremendous pain, even then, another message was being incepted into my tween brain: caring for others—even at the cost of your own well-being—is noble. It's something to be proud of.

This lesson was implanted by her without harmful intent, handed down from one generation to the next with a giggle and a hug. And I took it and carried it forward for years, believing that having my needs met wasn't the marker of a life well lived; that instead, meeting the needs of others, no matter how much it caused me to suffer, was where my pride should live.

The transformative influence of Aziz Joon's love on my life can't be understated, but she also accidentally implanted one of the most impactful limiting beliefs of my life. Notice that she did this without malice or even intent, but there it was. *Caring for others at a cost to yourself is something to be proud of.* This belief is what caused me to believe that my job was my mom's emotional care, stopping me from really ever stepping into my power.

As I got older and craved freedom, independence, time with my friends, and attention from boys, I only felt guilt. Those desires meant I wasn't a "good" girl who cared for my mom; they made me selfish. If I chased those desires, my mom would be lonely, and that made me "bad." When I decided to fulfill those desires, I accepted the label of "bad," and looked for evidence that this limiting belief was true.

Did I find it? Absolutely! From every adult around, I'd hear it repeatedly: "bad" or "lazy." I became the black sheep. I was caught between extremes. The little girl who sacrificed her own needs to take care of her mom's heart, and the rebellious kid who never did the right thing. Neither projection reflected who I was at my core, but they became my identity, nonetheless.

One of the cruel aspects of limiting beliefs is that we simply accept them as a truth of our existence. As children, we are unaware that these beliefs were implanted, that they are not our own, and that they are very outdated. As we grow, our limiting beliefs grow with us. For me, the belief that taking care of others at the cost of my own well-being extended from my relationship with my family to my friendships, to my romantic relationships, to my career. It followed me everywhere, reminding me constantly that if I wanted to be valuable, I needed to put others' needs before my own.

This touched every decision I made. I lived at home in college so my single mom wouldn't be lonely. I missed college parties so my boyfriend didn't feel left out. I said *yes* to people when I meant *no*, and *no* when I meant *yes*. I hid my opinion when I could feel other people's disapproval or lack of understanding. Most of all, I assimilated. Big-time. I wore my naturally curly hair straight. I switched the Persian music in the car to the radio the minute someone got in. I smiled, I nodded, I spoke softly and sweetly. I told my anger she had no right to take up space. Anything to make the person across from me comfortable with who I was.

Putting others' feelings before my own was only one of my limiting beliefs, but it motivated so much of what I did and who I was until it I couldn't bear it any longer. Until I hit a wall in the most profound and existential sense. But that is a story for another chapter.

The original experiencer of these traumas creates survival beliefs to survive their circumstances; my grandmother's belief system helped her do that. But the thing to remember is that those survival tools only work up to a certain point. When past generations hand us their belief systems, they do so without fully taking in the depth and breadth of who we are—and what our own, updated circumstances look like.

That is the funny part of passed-down belief systems; they can be hundreds of years old, and we still pull them out and put them to use, daily. Imagine using a telegraph to send a message to your friend instead of texting. Making decisions based on these passed-down, limiting beliefs is similar: it's applying outdated "technology" to our modern lives.

There is real, deep trauma—like war, oppression, disease and poverty—that creates these limiting beliefs in families, in societies, and in cultures. These limiting belief bodyguards are massive—they stand tall, and they protect ferociously because our pain is too great to bear. These beliefs are how our ancestors survived, which means the evidence is clear for them: these belief systems are in fact a life raft. They work! So, our ancestors wrap them gently and devotedly hand them down from one generation to the next.

This is never so apparent as it is with communities of people who have been ostracized by white colonial culture. Colonialism has harmed generations of people of color, queer people, working-class people, and women by telling us that who we are is not enough, by creating a white illusion of perfection that no one can attain, by erasing our humanity and introducing the deep shame that is born from being considered subhuman,

One of the most subversive forms of harm from colonial thinking has been a consistent attack on our intuition. As a means to control, we have been taught for hundreds of years that sensing is the enemy. That instead of sensing with our intuitive knowing, we should accept what we're being told by those attempting to accumulate power. Sensing is the enemy of anyone who is trying to control you, and it's followed us into our present. "You're too sensitive" is a dagger used to tell people that they're crazy, or at least irrational because they sense so deeply.

Remember the moment of disconnect from Higher Self? It continues from here. Demanding conformity, instilling normative beliefs to create perfect little boys and girls, demonizing desire, longing, uniqueness, differences, disagreement, dissent. Every time our ancestors became disconnected from their Higher Selves by this system, they suffered trauma. The biggest was the kind that said, *If you are not one of us, you can't exist at all.*

So, to survive, our ancestors assimilated. They gave up their deepest truths, their sharpest yearnings, their wild, gorgeous, primordial selves. In their place, they built limiting beliefs about who they had to be to stay safe, to belong, to simply exist. They handed each and every one of those beliefs right down to us. In addition to our own beliefs, we carry within us their limiting beliefs too.

The intention of our ancestors in handing us these limiting beliefs is never harm. The intention is survival. But what happens when those hard times our ancestors lived through have changed or need to change, and we are still in survival mode? When the survival voice is louder than the voice that wants us to thrive? We accept that trauma as unchangeable. It's not. These systems have outgrown themselves. They're killing us.

Knowing this, isn't it time to unwrap these packages disguised as gifts and see the pain that is actually hiding beneath, disguised as treasure? Isn't it time to gently set those beliefs down and begin to explore the power of our own truth in search of a new outcome? Don't we owe that not just to ourselves, but to those very same ancestors that fought with all their souls so that we might exist?

I think so. Thriving—not just for ourselves, but for them—is the least we can do to thank them for what they've given us. We can make their suffering the ultimate act of rebellion against systems of oppression that do not want to see us step into our power. What could be more powerful than learning to own your own narrative?

## *White Noise Drowns Out Higher Self*

Here is a fundamental truth about limiting beliefs: while they are present to protect the vulnerable, fearful parts of us, they make a hell of a lot of noise doing it. In intuition coaching, I call this **white noise**.

Basically, these disempowering beliefs become so loud that they disrupt the frequency of our Higher Self and its language of intuition. White noise makes it really damn hard to hear our own truth, what we know to be right for us, or even our truest desires. Still, intuition is not deterred. It continues to whisper, just like it did when we were little, but the distortion from the limiting beliefs is so loud, we can't hear it.

I have the wonderful privilege of coaching some well-known people, and I will say that even these maximally successful, rich, and even famous people struggle with limiting beliefs.

Hopefully this isn't too much of a surprise; we should all know by now that money, power, and acclaim aren't the keys to happiness. Can they make life more comfortable? Absolutely. But along with great achievements, they aren't the keys to overcoming lifelong insecurities and self-limitations. I think you would be surprised by how much limiting beliefs impact *everyone*. It's important to talk about this because the truth of the matter is that healing from limiting beliefs is the only way to find sustainable happiness.

One of my clients has been working hard on identifying how his limiting beliefs cause him to shrink in certain power dynamics. Even though he has millions of fans who see power and dignity in him, he freezes whenever he's in a situation where he has to advocate for himself against someone who he feels has authority over him. In our work, we've found that the white noise of his younger self, a tween who struggled as a queer person in small-town USA, can be so loud, so directive, that it's all he can hear in these moments.

*Back down! Just nod and smile! Please, whatever you do, don't make them look at us, don't stand out*, it pleads. His limiting belief is that his mere presence makes people uncomfortable, so what can he do but shrink?

When we do the work to heal these limiting beliefs, another voice comes rushing in. His Higher Self begins whispering: *Your purpose is to bring people joy. You can't bring joy when you give up your power. Show people they can have both. It's all in you, show them.*

In our work he started noticing something that became a powerful unlocking tool: when he acts from his Higher Self, people listen, even the ones with more power than him. When he acts in accordance with his limiting belief, he gets written off and ignored, without fail. This is the difficult and self-destructive part of limiting beliefs: they want to protect us, but they end up doing the opposite—they cause us to give up our power, which only creates more pain. Are you starting to see why it is so important to uproot them?

Some of my favorite awakenings to this truth are those in my clients who exist under the pressure of the public spotlight, because they have the most influence in shaping culture and thinking. One they get it, the ripple effect is enormous. These clients usually come to me during a public crisis that they are sure will end their career. To be fair, getting torn apart in the media—social media included—is *not* something that's easy to stay centered through. It is harsh, it is hurtful, and it is terrifying. Most of that experience of terror and pain comes from two limiting beliefs:

1. They are imposters and will eventually be found out, and;
2. Their mistakes make them disposable.

Those limiting beliefs are standing guard over even more terrified parts of them, the younger parts that believe they aren't valuable, talented, special, or redeemable. They believe that whatever mistake they make will reveal the truth to everyone: they aren't enough, they are an imposter. And that's a pretty common feeling for people, regardless of their public recognizability. It's scary to feel like you aren't enough, that if people figure out the "real" you, you'll be left behind.

The noise being projected by these beliefs is so loud that the fear voice takes the wheel and makes all the decisions. Their first instinct is to react from that fear, which either comes across as defensive or disengaged. They can't separate their own truth from the gossip being spread about them because the noise of these limiting beliefs is so loud that they are shut off to the guidance coming from their most powerful source of wisdom: Higher Self.

Higher Self can prioritize accountability while holding on to dignity. It understands that there is room for both making mistakes and being worthy of love. These are my favorite cases because when we do work with their fearful parts, quiet down these limiting beliefs, and finally reconnect them to that inner wisdom, the answers are so readily waiting for them. They don't need teams of PR people writing public statements or publicists telling them how to handle themselves; they have the answers within.

These people know exactly what to do, exactly how to tell their story, and when they do, every time, without fail, they turn what felt like a crisis into an opportunity to share their truth with the world and connect with people in a deeper way than ever before. It's like I always tell these clients: the truth will set you free, but first, you have to be willing to heal the shame that's hiding it from view.

### Reconstructing Our Beliefs

Am I capable of taking this job?

Am I worthy of this relationship?

Do I deserve to be treated this way?

Take a deep breath, and remember: These questions won't go away overnight. Maybe they won't ever fully disappear, but they also don't have to take up as much space in your life and in your decisions as they do today. The path toward repairing these broken, limiting beliefs about yourself starts by just witnessing them, and then slowly coming into dialogue with them. Becoming aware that they exist, understanding that they are implants from the outside, and gently questioning them, without judgment or shame, pulls them out of the darkness into the light of day. When we work with these parts, they quiet down and let Higher Self speak.

The good news is this: Your Higher Self never goes away, and its communication to you through your intuition never stops. The whispering is always there, you just have to clear the noise of the limiting beliefs to hear it. Know this: any belief that limits you is not coming from your Higher Self, it is not your innate truth.

If a belief feels limiting, it was incepted into you. If a seed has been planted it can definitely be uprooted. Healing starts with identifying your limiting beliefs, looking at them head-on, and seeing them for what they are: other people's limitations masquerading as your truth. That awareness alone will dislodge their roots and give you room to heal and clear them from your life.

The work of healing limiting beliefs is the work of a lifetime. Mine started the day I met Rhea, my mentor. She's a gifted healer and yes, she is an intuitive. She just knows things. You'll hear so much more about her because she's been pivotal in my journey of coming into my own truth and doing the work I do. She's the first person to tell me that I too had these gifts and she's worked with me tirelessly over the past decade to unearth them.

Like I said, this is lifelong work. All of my clients are still in the process of identifying and uprooting their limiting beliefs, as am I. You will learn about new beliefs every day. Even when you are reconnected and living joyfully in concert with Higher Self, you will sometimes find that white noise creeps in, drowning out the messages you need most.

The limiting beliefs springing forward from within at the tender age when you are emerging out of your early childhood and getting ready to take on the world as a teenager set up the most perfect conditions for an epic battle. We'll work on the multistep process of healing in section three, but for now you're an adolescent. Soon your Higher Self will come out swinging, challenging the limiting beliefs that have been instilled in you. But who will win?

EXPLORATION: *Your Greatest Wish*

Let's identify a specific limiting belief. You might be thinking, *I've been to therapy—I can rationalize my way through self-limiting talk*, or, *How would I even begin to identify the deepest root of a limiting belief if I wasn't even aware of when it got planted in me?* Here's a start:

Think about something you want deep within your soul. This should be a desire you wouldn't willingly share with anybody, or, if you did, you would be embarrassed by it. Hint: if you're embarrassed by this desire, it's a good one for this exercise. For me it's to be the next Oprah... I'm talking that level of embarrassing to say out loud.

Now, envision a stage with a single microphone and one spotlight. Go ahead and invite the inner fear voice that doesn't believe your wish is possible or realistic to the spotlight or microphone. Give them the prompt: "Tell me why this thing I want is impossible." Invite the voice to give you all the reasons why. As they speak, write down every reason you get.

Awareness of this dynamic and dialogue is the first step to healing. How do you feel being told that your deepest desire is ridiculous, shameful, and impossible? Are you resentful? Rebellious? Ashamed? To what extent does your smallest self agree with the reasons that are being told to you?

Look at that list of reasons again, and now really ask yourself: *What evidence do I have this is true?*

Not just a feeling, but *evidence*.

Usually, in my experience, there's none.

This is a skill we are going to learn in depth in another chapter, but for now, I want you to remind yourself that other people's life experiences are not your evidence. Evidence is something that has happened in your life to you. Not to your mother. Not to your grandmother. Not to the kindergarten teacher or vocal coach or first boss or college professor who didn't see your gifts.

Finally, ask yourself: *Why do I want to believe I am not worthy of my deepest desire? That it is not possible? How does this protect me?* Just note for yourself whatever comes up.

As I said before, your self-imposed limitations are not trying to hurt you; they were implanted to protect you. But hopefully your most rebellious self knows that these limiting beliefs are bullshit. Speaking of rebellion, I think it's time to remind you of a part of yourself that was most connected to your Higher Self: you as a teenager.

Meet you there.

CHAPTER 4

# My Teenage Hero

T*here's a reason the teenage* era is dramatized, immortalized, and idolized in pop culture—it's *intense*. After years of hiding your truth to gain parental validation, and bottling the wild, weird, and wonderful, suddenly, as a teenager, it's time for you to focus on you again . . . which means you have to make space. And you are not going to do it quietly.

Slowly, the people that raised you fade into the background. Their ideas, needs, and expectations become less urgent, less linked to your survival. In the expanse that opens, your Higher Self perks up. Your Higher Self knows that in this stage of your evolution, individuating is essential to your growth, so it morphs. It expands the gentle curiosity it embodied in your tiny self to a more passionate, emboldened, hungrier version of itself.

*Break away*, it says.

*Know yourself*, it insists.

You have to answer the call, and to do that, you have to go at it alone. You drift into your room, over to the mirror or your phone. You drift even as the fearful, disappointed faces in your house plead with you to go back to the kid they once knew. As you drift away, you feel the intoxicating energy of freedom creep in.

And yet, as Higher Self infuses the elixir of freedom throughout your veins, your human self continues to have needs, and those needs are growing too. Belonging is still a part of what makes you feel whole. You can't belong at home, but you must belong somewhere.

*Go ahead, jump,* says Higher Self.

So, you gather yourself and leap from the great big steamship that is your family to the shiny, bright, dizzying speedboat whizzing past. Your focus becomes your friends, kindred spirits pulled together by the same magnetic call: *know yourself.*

## Addicted to Validation

When I was fifteen, I was groomed by a man twelve years older than me. He was a friend of the family and we all found him to be absolutely intriguing; charming, worldly, and hilarious. Over the course of that summer, he'd come to dinner at least twice a week, making my mom, sister, and me hang on his every word with his cinematic stories of escaping Iran, living in Paris alone as a teenager, and finally making a life in the US. He turned our lonely home into a dazzling circus full of excitement and anticipation.

I'm not sure how it happened. I found him so glorious, I could hardly believe he existed. As an awkward teenager, I was sure he spent about as much time thinking about me as a fish does a bicycle. Then, out of the blue, during one of his visits that summer, he began to take an interest in me.

At the time, my feelings about myself amounted to two words: *not enough.* I felt like I was hideous with my frizzy hair, compared to all the cheerleaders with their gleaming blond hair. My clothes, which we bought on sale wherever we could afford, did not have any special labels on them, and they definitely weren't trendy. It wasn't much better at home, where the constant comparison to my much more studious and hardworking sister left only one plausible conclusion for my family: I was lazy.

One thing was working in my favor. For the first time in my life, that summer I discovered I wanted something more than I wanted to make my mom and sister happy. Suddenly their sadness, which I had taken on like carry-on luggage, started to feel foreign to me. The accusations that my apathy toward studying and cleaning made me appalling because I didn't gleefully pick up a book or a mop started to feel like clothes that just didn't fit.

I started to hear my own inner voice again: *You are more than that*, it would say, and at fifteen, I started to believe it.

Well, almost believe it.

I believed it enough to reject my family's projections and start to notice there was a cyclone of wants and needs inside that I had ignored. That push from my Higher Self made me look beyond what my family thought or needed and made me notice myself again. That was a start, but I also had my own baggage to wade through: a father who had been absent for the past seven years, a deep need to be desired as an awkward girl who never got any attention from boys her age, and a desperate yearning to get out of that stuffy house that made me feel poor, unworthy, and small. Not knowing there existed such a thing as Higher Self or inner wisdom, what I did instead is let the attention of that man twelve years my senior become the beacon out of that dark place, which I exuberantly followed.

Eighteen months of chaos came crashing down on me from that one choice. I lost my connection to my family, my one life raft, overnight. My mom begged me to stop; she tried threatening me with groundings, to which I'd shout, "I'll just run away!" She worried and cried and pleaded. I aged her ten years in that time. My sister completely stopped speaking to me. My extended family would toggle between trying to talk sense into me and feeling uncomfortable in my presence, isolating me in a world of polite smiles and awkward looks.

I was so embarrassed to take this grown man around my teenage friends, I became alienated from them, and any kids my age, and I was stuck in a new trap: a possessive boyfriend who used his age and authority to mold me to fit his needs. He'd tell me I didn't need any of those people anyway. That no one understood me like he did. He'd promise a big life; he'd get his degree, we'd move to a beautiful house together, and I could finally feel safe financially. I thought my life was finally becoming everything I'd dreamed of: safe, with the love of a man, and full of interesting new experiences and people.

Those flashes of hope didn't last very long. We would be walking through the mall, and he'd imagine me and a young boy my age exchanging glances and things would get dark. Broken dishes, screaming fights, stinging slaps across my face. Who could I turn to in those moments? I couldn't go back to my family, tail between my legs, after fighting against them so hard. Besides, I wasn't really sure they loved me anymore. Their iciness filled me with shame.

I'd ride it out, it would get better. I had proof this was true once the flowery apologies started. Promises, poems, tears, vowing to never harm me again. He'd say I was the most precious thing in his life—and because he was the only one saying that to me, it drew me back in. And the cycle would start over.

This went on until I heard the familiar voice of my Higher Self again in October of my junior year of high school. That fall, I met Pam, Mano, and Ernesto in class, three people who quickly became my three best friends, and being with them changed everything. Riding around in Pam's old 4Runner, singing "One Drop" by Bob Marley from the top of our lungs, and skipping English to go to Starbucks just to hear the barista play his guitar during his smoke breaks felt like a dizzying gallop toward freedom.

*This is it!* the voice said from inside. *This iss the out you've been really looking for. Run toward this!*

Just because I heard this voice and felt its intoxicating pull toward my liberation didn't mean I didn't also hear my fear self screaming at me from the other side about how unloved and lonely I would be if I left my toxic relationship.

That fear voice is so convincing, but once you've learned the lesson from whatever circumstance your fear self kept you in, the time for that circumstance to come to its end arrives. That's when you open back up again to that magnetic pull from Higher Self.

That gave me the courage to feel my fear but to keep trudging forward, through it, toward the dizzying sense of freedom Higher Self was dangling in front of me. My freedom, my expansion, became more intoxicating than the safety of my fearful, small self that felt I needed to do whatever it took to be loved.

So, at seventeen, I left the guy behind, and I started to chase that feeling.

And it saved my life.

In my case, meeting that particular group of friends is what reminded me of my Higher Self and made me want to embody her again, but it can work both ways for teens. As you move from your family being the focus of your attention to your friends, belonging with this group matters more than anything.

If this group of friends doesn't love us for living our truth, Higher Self will remain the enemy and we'll shy away from it again. Even though we shed our need for our family's validation to some extent, we don't shed the limiting beliefs they and our childhood experiences instilled in us. The result is that we replace the need for our parents' validation with the need for our peers' validation.

There's an inherent issue of basing who we are on the opinions of people who are also in the process of learning who they are: *everyone* is confused. That foggy mirror doesn't reflect our truth, our value, or our Higher Self. It instead reflects back all the angst, the confusion, and the limiting beliefs of the people who are growing up and figuring out who they are alongside us.

But we don't know that (at least at the time), so we decide that to hold value, we must fit in. In the midst of all this confusion, someone undoubtedly emerges who projects the most confidence in the group, and we follow them. We group together, dressing like they do, talking like they do, liking the things they like so that we too can shine as bright. Once again Higher Self's passionate calls turn into whispers as the noise of fitting in and getting validation from others becomes loudest.

After I entered the relationship with this man, I didn't really pay attention to my Higher Self again until a year later, and again, only when peers entered the picture and I wanted their stamp of approval instead of his.

Stop now and think: Looking back on your teen years, what images come to mind?

> What were you doing most?
>
> How did you spend time?
>
> Most important, how did you feel about yourself?
>
> How did your limiting beliefs about yourself become louder in high school?
>
> Do you remember how you took care of those vulnerabilities?
>
> What concessions did you make to fill the void those limiting beliefs left in you?

The coping strategies you developed as a teen still live within you, and, when you are in pain or stress, they jump in to protect you. That's what they have been trained to do. You've just been taught to name those aspects things like *anxiety, fear, imposter syndrome* rather than *my fifteen-year-old self, my eighteen-year-old self*, and so on. The limiting beliefs we discussed in the last chapter are watered and take root in new ways—and, as we become adults, make decisions for us more often than we'd expect.

I have a client who is an executive leader at an illustrious fashion brand. She and I work together on learning how to trust her boundaries with other people, how not to let others' chaos become her own. We practice not playing nice to make other people more comfortable, which is hard for many of the female-identifying executives I coach.

But why do we need so much practice? The truth is that there isn't a thirty-something executive in the driver's seat when boundaries are being crashed, there's a fourteen-year-old in charge who is desperate to be liked. She's the one deciding what to say and do based on an old limiting belief she created at that age. *We have to make sure people like us,* says this younger self. *It's more important than anything,* including her own needs. That doesn't work when you're leading a team. But when we don't stop to identify who is making those decisions within and give them some space and attention, they continue to drive the car and push us, and our Higher Self, into the passenger seat.

When I can feel these younger selves taking the wheel, I will stop a coaching session and do a visualization exercise with my clients. With this specific client, when I ask her to envision her younger self, she closes her eyes and always sees the same image: her fourteen-year-old self sitting on her own in her high school cafeteria feeling misunderstood.

There is always a story behind that kind of image. My client is the child of an irresponsible father, who took away the feeling of security from the family, and a mother prone to anxiety and despair over his actions. That made my client's job as a child the bringer of levity. She had to always be jovial and happy, even if that wasn't how she felt. As a six- or seven-year-old child, she believed that her parents were better if she was around to lift them up. Her dad wouldn't make that immature decision, her mom would smile, her brother would be distracted from the chaos. A core belief of hers became that if she could make people happy, she was safe. Understanding what she wanted wasn't important.

Since her value became about what she brought to other people, she became unable to see what value she had on her own. In only existing to make others happy, there was a disconnect with friends who knew what they wanted or who they wanted to be. Her self-image was contingent on the opinions of others, and so, she was naturally not understood. How could she be? She didn't even understand herself.

Whenever there is a disconnect between her present self, the high-powered executive, and the decisions she is making, my client and I know it is time to travel backward. We always go back to that cafeteria where she's sitting alone, feeling unseen. That wound is alive and well in her.

And even though there are times that wounded aspect wants to call the shots today, she's learned that instead of following its terrified guidance, instead she can soothe that self by speaking her truth. She tells me lately how this simple reframe has allowed her to feel so much more empowered but also allowed more compassion for others in her leadership, making her connections to people profoundly deeper and more impactful.

### The Nesting Doll: Limiting Beliefs Meet Shame

This is the difficulty of the teenage years. We begin to play out the limiting beliefs we have been handed in our homes or other early communities. We are like a nesting doll of fears incepted in us. At the core is the child with the original wound; the next layer is the teenage self, who lives out the next chapter of the limiting belief. Our core wound never leaves us, but it does begin to take on new dimensions as each iteration of our selves tries it on and walks out into the world. Thus, the core wound of our childhood is amplified by an entirely new emotion brought out during adolescence: **shame**.

Now, teens have a bad rep for being judgy. But to me, judgment is less a sign of how someone feels about other people and more a sign of how that person feels about themselves. Usually, these judgmental people are also being deeply hard on themselves. Rather than admitting shame over what you feel is lacking in your own life, it is easier to project judgment onto others. (For many people, this tendency carries well into adulthood.)

That ease of projection is why our teenage years are some of the most judgmental and shame-filled years we can experience. Just like our little selves build limiting beliefs to manage the pain, so do these teen aspects. They too make decisions about who they need to be or what they need to give up to gain love and acceptance.

One of my clients talks to me often about her codependence on others, and we work on bringing in her Higher Self to remove this addiction to others' attention and approval. But we'll often get interrupted by another voice who pulls at her during our sessions. Higher Self will be flowing through with incredible, empowering messages. Then, bam! Suddenly it will disappear, and she can't hear it anymore. Ideas like *Yeah, but if you aren't in this relationship you won't find anyone better* start coming through.

"Who's that?" I'll ask.

When we take a minute and close our eyes, we see her. She's sixteen, an artist and a rebel, and her teachers, parents, and coaches are exasperated with her. They want her to be a certain way, to be less spontaneous and more controlled. They want to have an easier time "managing" her. Their message is: *You're not enough unless you stop being less of who you are.* But her friends see her. The boys who want to date her, they do a good job making her feel like enough. In their midst, she is more than enough. Without them, she's left with the shame and the judgmental voices that tell her if she wants to be worthy, she *has* to be more disciplined.

This sort of identification is critical to the work in reuniting my clients with their Higher Self. Once we can see that the beliefs she's currently operating under come from this sixteen-year-old who is confusing the attention of her friends with the acceptance she craved from her parents, we're able to separate her present self from those beliefs. We're able to give that sixteen-year-old the attention she's been craving, and in doing so, not only do we heal this aspect, but we get the inner teenager to calm her persistent warnings, decreasing the noise she's creating in my client's life. I say this to my clients all the time: "You are who your younger self has been waiting for. They just want to be witnessed by you."

This work of taking care of a younger part of self *is* what opens space for the wiser voice to break through. By identifying the beliefs that came from a teenager, we become aware of how those old beliefs, created by a much younger, shame-filled version of us, still influences our decisions today. That awareness will allow you to make room for Higher Self to reinsert its guidance and create a more centered, rooted strategy than the one a younger version would have you use out of a place of pain and self-doubt. We will learn to do this work in detail in a later chapter, but it is useful to begin thinking back to your teenage selves now as we begin to unpack the beliefs they formed.

Our teenage selves were justified to create the strategies for survival they did. In our teen years, our friends offer us a pathway out of the shame adults create in us, and yet they have a whole host of judgments about themselves that get projected onto us. It is a cruel sort of trap we get stuck in—finding solace from the judgment we see in the adults around us only to be judged by the people who we believe will be our saviors.

This is where the need for validation begins to become an *addiction*. I call it **validation addiction** because it becomes a need we will do pretty much anything to have met. Our parents are right to worry in some ways; our decisions are motivated by this addiction and the shame underneath it. This is how peer pressure is possible—we will do anything for that hit.

### *A Quick Detour to the Land of Likes and Shares*

The effect of social media on teens (and all of us) is no secret. There is plenty of discourse out there about how it has impacted our ability to build intimacy and its effect on self-esteem. Watching my own kids go into teendom, I can see how validation addiction has exploded because of TikTok, Snapchat, and Instagram. Teens are primed to make these platforms successful, because they're already looking for likes (or being liked) as a way to measure their value.

Mark Zuckerberg wasn't far from being a teenager himself when he dreamt up Facebook, his own teenage yearning for other people's likes driving a vision that has ingrained in us the way we think about popularity today. The currency of followers and likes as a sign of value and popularity is only possible because we're preprogrammed to crave validation. In teens, it's the perfect storm: a teenager's natural inclination to shape their identity based on people's opinions meets platforms that monetize that desire.

The conversation about validation is louder than ever thanks to social media. But does villainizing the platform solve the issue of validation? I say an emphatic *no* to that question. I think these platforms allow us to fully see the extent and impact of validation in our culture. Think about the conversations we can have with teens from that place of awareness about the value of a like over the value of their own truth, needs, and well-being.

These are conversations that parents of millennials or boomers couldn't have had with their kids. I don't think we fully understood validation addiction before social media. Social media is like a glaring flashlight that's allowed us to look at our behaviors more closely and hopefully help guide our kids.

Through this new level of awareness, my hope is that conversations can open up between parents and their teens about how we've been taught to judge our value versus the reality of where our value is actually sourced. They don't have to be awkward; you can simply start by asking things like:

*Do you believe that person on Instagram is showing their whole life?*

*How does it feel when something you make is liked and shared? Not liked or shared?*

*Do these people on this platform really know you? What don't they know about you?*

*If the college or employer of your dreams looked at what you're putting online five years from now, would you be proud of how it represents you?*

I'm saying this next statement fully aware of the age of divisiveness we now live in and how social media has contributed to it. But the truth is social media has spawned the greatest age of self-expression in our history. How many different platforms are there to express yourself today? Through photos, videos, words . . . in whatever way fits you. While it's addictive and enables validation and lets people live in their tiny echo chamber of like-minded people, it is also an enormous chance for all of us, especially teens, to express ourselves.

We need to take the good with the bad on this one. I work with some of today's most influential members of the queer and trans community—Alok, Jonathan van Ness, Dylan Mulvaney—all of whom have millions of followers, many of whom say that having access to someone living their truth so publicly has saved their lives.

Self-expression is the greatest path toward our inner truth, and these platforms are enabling it. Yes, they also enable projection, judgment, and false narratives, but whether we use them for good or for evil depends on where we are in our healing journeys.

### The Battle

Whether it was through social media or some other form of seeking validation from your peers, one thing remains true about your teen years: the battle between your inner truth and your need for others' acceptance begins to play out.

This may have caused you to reject all sorts of systems that were conditioning you to conform. This is where Higher Self exists, in the rejection of other people's truths and systems. Just like my client who was told her bucking of the system made her difficult, many of you had adults in your life who saw this Higher Self–driven rejection of their norms as **rebellion.**

Rebellion doesn't look the same in each person. It can show up in little ways, like simply choosing the opposite of what our parents do, or in big ways: running away, trying dangerous things, fighting any form of authority, or in my case, devoting my attention to a narcissistic groomer who had no business being in my life. Whether you rebelled quietly or fought like hell, like me, what you were doing in this act of rebellion was embodying your dignity, a major hallmark of Higher Self. Fighting for the dignity to express and understand yourself is 100 percent a Higher Self move.

You went through this process and persisted beyond the judgment of the adults in your life, for the most part. But how would it have been if you were taught that you had wisdom inside you? Would you have explored other things in life? Would you have made "stupid" decisions a little more safely?

> *Would you have drunk so much at that high school party where you barely knew anyone?*
>
> *Would you have tried pot for the first time with people you didn't feel safe with?*
>
> *Would you have said yes to having sex for the first time when what you really meant was no?*

If you had learned to trust the wisdom within, maybe you would have drunk or smoked that joint, but maybe you'd do it in the safety of a home or with a group of people you could trust. Maybe you would have said no when you meant no. What if you had been told, *Go, figure out who you are, trust the wisdom that's inside you?* Would you have had to rebel so fiercely?

Instead of being judged, what I wish is that we had been taught that our desire to push the boundaries is a natural part of our growth. I wish that we were reminded that we had deep wisdom guiding us. What if we had been guided to ask ourselves:

> *What do you really want?*
>
> *What are your ideas about this?*
>
> *How are these ideas different from what your friends think?*

Would we have been as addicted to validation if we had learned then that our own internal measuring stick held all the approval we were ever looking for?

I learned to start seeing things this way thanks to my own teenage daughter. Reina is a force of nature. She's been that way since she looked at me at the age of two and said, "NO! Mom! Reina don't like that!"

She's always known what she wanted, and she approaches most

things with a steady, rooted stance of assuredness. There's not a lot of swaying Reina or convincing her to play small for the sake of others. She just cannot do it, which I admire deeply.

Even though I like to see myself as an enlightened parent, practicing what I preach, I'd be lying if I said there haven't been times I asked her do things another way. Mostly this shows up in her strong stance with her peers. She is clear about which of their actions fit her truth and which do not, and she makes it known.

> She'll say no to plans that don't light her up.
>
> She'll move away from friends who don't make her feel fully seen.
>
> She'll let people know—real quick—if they've disrespected her in any way.

Pretty badass for a fifteen-year-old, right?

Well, I hate to admit that this used to make me *so* uncomfortable. But my discomfort, I realized, wasn't coming from the version of me that's rooting for her as her mom; it was coming from my own inner fifteen-year-old who would have done absolutely anything to be liked.

*How can she be so brazen?* I catch this inner teen of mine saying.

Not being able to stand it any longer, my inner fifteen-year-old would pipe up, asking Reina why she doesn't just back down, give people more leeway, give them a third and fourth chance. The mom in me sees it differently, but it's true that sometimes the kids around us trigger us back to the version of ourselves at that same age.

Reina's staunch stance in her views and attaining her needs knocked me out of that limited place of validation. She reminded me, just by existing so fully as who she is, that other people's needs don't ever matter more than hers. She keeps showing me what being aligned to my powerful Higher Self could have looked like when I was fifteen, and I marvel at her every day for it.

Does she struggle from time to time? Of course. She's human like the rest of us. Sometimes she needs validation too, but I notice that instead of throwing herself into the deep end, she'll dip her toe in and see pretty quickly what does and doesn't align with her. Maybe it's because she's being raised by someone who wants that for her and talks to her about it incessantly, much to her boredom and dismay. But I can't take nearly all the credit. There's also something in Reina that is unwaveringly . . . Reina. She's always been my teacher in this way.

Not all of us have Reina's ability to stand strong. Most of us needed that validation from our friends, but while we were chasing that, we were doing something really important: we were individuating from our family.

This is a survival skill we have to learn, so this individuation is a part of nature. Our parents don't necessarily see it that way, which makes our relationship with them strained during adolescence, but it also invites in new cheerleaders, new adults who see our truth and push us toward living it. Teachers, coaches, parents of friends, other relatives; as teenagers we start to forge new bonds with adults, looking for those who see and support us. Through this guidance, we can turn them back toward their own internal compass, knowing that they too have a Higher Self that will guide them toward their truth, teaching them to trust this voice above all else.

After all, teens are in a bit of a lose-lose situation. They need to individuate and develop their own ideas to grow, and yet if they reject the ideals put upon them by their families and by society, they are considered treacherous. It becomes a paradox: we don't take their acts of rebellion seriously enough, and we simultaneously take them far too seriously.

Reframing your own teenage years can be helpful. What if your teenage self wasn't some irrational, dangerous rebel? What if your teenage self was the first time you really looked at the limitations, judgment, and self-hatred being handed to you and firmly put your foot down? Seen this way, your teenage self appears deeply heroic in the battle for your soul.

Rebellion should be our sign that we are following our journey, that we are reacquainting ourselves with our inner wisdom. Instead of being zombified, we are following a path that's being defined by a newly forming inner compass. We aren't supposed to follow the path others set for us, and yet the world is so offended when we don't. Our attempts to self-actualize are messaged as an inconvenience, and we wind up feeling that we should value praise and being "good" in other people's opinion more than whatever voice exists within.

The adults around us tell us, through this judgment, that we don't have any inner wisdom. We are told that wisdom is earned through age and experience, and in that way our innate wisdom is dismissed—along with our Higher Self—altogether. Even worse, we are beginning to be subjected to forces far greater and more organized—education, the media, and capitalism—which see our Higher Selves as their opposition.

But before we go there, stop for a second and savor the wild rebellion of you in these years. Feel your soul pulsing through as you came to know yourself through your desire. That moment, felt right now, is probably the closest you've been to Higher Self until today.

### EXPLORATION: *A Homage to the Hero*

If you relate to seeing your teenage self weighed down by unfair labels and judgments, I want you to take a moment now and imagine that version of yourself breaking free of those bonds. See your teenage self truly as they were, working hard to help you figure out your values and your dreams. We're going to do this together now.

What was your favorite song or album when you were sixteen? Go find it and put it on.

While you listen, sit down and write a letter to your sixteen-year-old self, using these prompts:

HI [NAME],

    I'm writing to thank you. To thank you for . . .

You were incredible at . . .

Sometimes our parents/family didn't understand you when you . . .

That's because they were trying to protect you, or themselves. You actually were wise to push in those ways because it made us (stronger, happier, etc.).

So, I want to thank you for pushing in those ways. Because you overcame those pressures, I am now able to . . .

I know being accepted by others is still important to you because it makes you feel . . .

But I want you to know we're working on something new, on finding our inner wisdom and accepting ourselves, and that includes you.

So let me end this letter by telling you all the reasons you're incredible so that you know that I see you and admire every part of you.

To end the letter, list a few things here that made your sixteen-year-old self so awesome. Try to think about it from the perspective of both selves. What did you think made you awesome then? What would you think made sixteen-year-old you awesome now?

PART II

# The Crisis of Disconnection

CHAPTER 5

# The World Around You

*Limiting beliefs have been wreaking* havoc since the beginning of time. They are ingrained in our culture and as we leave teenagerhood and become adults, we walk into a world full of them. Your limiting beliefs have been given an invitation to be louder than your own intuitive wisdom by a lot of **systems** around you: the media, capitalism, organized religion, higher education—the list goes on.

> This has been the story since the beginning of time Here are a few gems from history:
>
> Gladiator blood will cure epilepsy.
>
> Applying leeches to the body is the best cure for yellow fever and laryngitis.
>
> A mental disorder called drapetomania is what causes Black slaves to flee captivity.

Are these things true? Of course not. We can say with certainty from our current vantage point that they are not only ridiculous, but some are also deeply problematic. But, if you were living in 200 B.C., 1710, or 1841, calling these assertions ridiculous would get you ousted from society. What changed between then and now? Back in the day, these ideas were commonly believed, and the common acceptance of an idea is what took it from opinion to fact.

When we look back at these ideas, we know that believing them made people do and say things that were dangerous to themselves and dehumanizing to others. But had you lived back then, you would have done the same, because, well, who can argue with the truth, right? And, even if you did think the ideas were crazy, was saying so worth the societal price you would pay?

To me, the most notable part of this whole construct is that we have thousands of years of evidence showing us how blindly accepting certain beliefs as truth has ... well, created disastrous results. This is why I'm completely obsessed with history. If you walk into my house on Saturday morning, you'll see me doing some household chore with the History Channel on. If I'm out on a walk or a hike, there's a history podcast in my ear. If you walk into my office, you will find more books on history than on any other topic, including spirituality and psychology.

History is the most tangible evidence for how our beliefs block or free us. History shows us the folly of our own convictions. It reveals how we as humans fall wholeheartedly into beliefs that define our actions. All of that is juicy material for an intuition coach, but studying history shows me that for centuries, power structures have used one idea to stay in power: that when you control "truth," you control the masses.

My total and complete infatuation with history started thanks to my eleventh-grade history teacher, Mrs. Penn. She was a woman with a booming voice and a large presence. She told us about history like a story that unfolded bit by bit every time we would sit down in her classroom. Walking up and down the aisle of desks and chairs, her big wooden bangles clunking together, she would painstakingly teach us about every religion around the world and how their similarities and differences created both unity and deep separation in humanity.

Every time she would tell us about a belief from ancient history that we found to be preposterous, she would look at us seriously and say, "Honey, there's only one thing to remember: if you believe it, then it's true." She was using that lesson to teach us that throughout history, every crusade or war was fought by people who truly believed in the cause, regardless of whether history proved them wrong. Belief alone made their cause their reality.

Without some common acceptance of what truth actually is, people who want power are able to divide us by popularizing their versions of truth. People lose their lives, families stop speaking, and shit gets bad. So, where's the line? How do we stay awake to the desire of systems to divide and control us by defining the "truth" for us? How do we instead cocreate what is true by welcoming and honoring our inner wisdom? Understanding the nuance between our truth and others' is a hard one, but we are prepared for it. We come built with the intelligence to navigate this thin tightrope. Mmm-hmm . . . we have Higher Self.

You Higher Self is continuously whispering to you; we've established this. Your limiting beliefs from childhood, aspects of you that are stuck in pain or trauma and still trying to protect you, also speak to you. Most of the time they are louder than Higher Self. Now I get to tell you the *real* reason they have permission to be louder. Now we will look at the environment surrounding us and how that environment encourages our limiting beliefs to be the loudest voice within us.

The media, capitalism, education and culture are all deeply influential systems that prey on our limiting beliefs. These structures want you to give into your limiting beliefs to create more fear; fear keeps us desperate; desperation seeks guidance, validation, and an answer. What better environment to sell, control, and accumulate power than one built off fear and desperation?

### Structure 1: Media

Don't believe me yet? Let's break it down. Consider the media. When's the last time you turned on the news? When you did that, how did you feel? Were you showered with hope and a sense of possibility? Did you feel good about humanity? Did you feel that we are all one and that working together is the best way to thrive?

Yeah, I didn't think so.

You probably felt dread, separation, anxiety, and, of course, fear. News is not just neutral; news is actually just *bad* news. You're being pumped with bad news all day long. Bad news after bad news. Does anything good happen in the world? Or is it happening so rarely that we don't hear about good news often?

*No!* Good things are happening every day, all around us, but a hit of hope doesn't get you hooked the way a hit of fear does. You know why? Because we're preprogrammed. That's right: here come those limiting beliefs again. They've been there with us since we first felt rejected for our truth. Since we were first told to sit down, shut up, do less, do more, be better. Our limiting beliefs created an environment of fear, so when we need to pay attention, fear gets our attention.

No one knows this better than the media. This becomes a cycle. Our fear sprouts up from our limiting beliefs within, media tell those fearful beliefs they are right, so they grow, big, and we pay more attention to the news, because the media tell our fears they are well-founded. The invitation for fear to get louder than our inner wisdom is there in every headline, news alert, and exposé. In the end, media decide what is real and what isn't.

That authority that we give the media troubles me. The media are full of self-proclaimed "experts," those who lack the background, experience, or training to provide valuable guidance, who are constantly spouting opinions that we treat as fact. In some ways, I think we have developed an overreliance on experts without demanding of ourselves that the final say must come from checking in with our own intuition.

Of course, there are people who genuinely have real expertise—health care providers, historians, researchers—whose input can help us learn and discern. But this new world of media has disconnected us from our own inner wisdom. It is still built on the idea that authority exists outside of us, that someone else knows better about our needs than we do. When we're presented with this sort of dichotomy, we usually choose to believe others' views, because we've been taught that we need validation from the external before we can trust what's coming from the internal.

Think about all of the content online promising to help you become more successful. Clickbait articles like *Five Tips to Be a Millionaire by 30*, news clips of business owners who say they don't sleep, never stop working, drink seven cups of coffee a day. The messages are always the same: *Push, strive, don't stop, just keep producing*. It's hustle culture, which doesn't allow you time to process big changes or to center and check in with your own needs. Hustle culture is about *doing*. Comparatively, the process of accessing inner wisdom is too quiet, too focused on just being. With media, it's often the loudest voice who wins out.

Culturally, this is true as well. We align our value with what we make and what we do with our time, not who we are on the inside. Without even realizing it, you may see headlines like the one above and immediately compare your own routine and decide you fall short. Right there you are reminded you are not enough. If instead the media were designed to teach you how to quiet the noise, quell the fear, heal the limiting beliefs that cause you to believe you're not enough in the first place, then, and only then, would media become truly empowering to you. In its current form, you are taught to rely on others' authority as the pathway to self-actualization.

You see the oxymoron here? How can you become more you, more self-actualized, by going away from yourself and toward the ideas of others? It doesn't work.

Self-actualization is about listening to our inner voice. It's about remembering who we are, really. Remembering that we are the same as our Higher Self, full of infinite wisdom and endless possibility. The media, both traditional and new, doesn't buy into that, not because it's foolish to believe we have a Higher Self, but because it pays to move us away from listening to our intuition and become totally reliant on outside sources for guidance and validation.

But what they're selling is a narrow and negative view. Your job is to remember to check in with your inner voice before taking the word of talking heads and self-appointed gurus at face value.

Here's the one thing you can do today to fight against this first system that's asking for your conformity: Check in with yourself when you take in its messages. How do you really feel after you watch or hear something in the media?

Ask questions about the news you read and the headlines that are regurgitated at you. Check in with that wise voice within and simply ask, *Does this resonate with me?* Remember that dissent is one of the greatest tools ever used for changing things that needed changing. History's greatest icons changed society for the better through dissent. Just before being assassinated in Memphis, Martin Luther King turned his attention from fighting segregation in the South to reminding white people in the North that their silence in the face of racism was the same as the violence and segregation happening in the South. This was counter to the popular narrative in the media at the time, casting Southerners as the only people in the US who were contributing to the problem of racism. King's dissent was radical. He made enemies from speaking this truth, but it was a truth we needed to face if we ever wanted to change.

Pulitzer Prize–winning author of *The Color Purple*, Alice Walker, once said, "The only way we will change the outcome of our global predicament is to change our understanding of what we have considered 'reality.' Change the tall tales of yesteryear that have always stymied and confused us. I am beyond weary, and most of the planet is, of the old explanations for our wretched plight as humans and the 'wisdom' hidden in enforced doctrines that are supposed to 'enlighten' us."[1]

This is the invitation to truth I'm asking us all to open ourselves to when we find ourselves face-to-face with media. Change comes from saying yes to this invitation rather than sleepwalking through whatever narrative is being spoon-fed to us to help keep the norms norming.

### Structure 2: Capitalism

One of the biggest systems that impact us is capitalism. Why is that? Because it makes us aware of where we're lacking.

*You are not enough as you are*, those voices yell at us. *But there's something you can buy to fix that . . .*

Just like with fear and the media, your limiting beliefs create the perfect environment for businesses to sell to you. You're told you just need this skin cream or hair dye or laptop or car or decor for your home, and *then* you'll be enough. You'll be happy. I worked in PR and marketing for twenty years—believe me, this is how the game works.

Forget my experience. Here I am writing this book and I just bought $75 undereye cream the other day because "they" told me aging is NOT OKAY. I'm a woman, after all, and getting older is not acceptable. Even if you know how these messages work against you, it's tough not to give in sometimes.

Don't get me wrong. Many of these products serve a need. Some of them even work! But when we believe they are essential to our worth, that the big house makes us more important than so-and-so down the street, or the nice car makes us more valuable than our friend from high school, we're giving in to the cycle. You should have those things because you love them, because the experience of engaging with them is fun or beautiful. Because that same soulful entity from your childhood wants that experience to expand and grow.

If you buy something because you're being told you're not

enough without it, the invitation to engage limiting beliefs gets even louder. By making those voices louder we're making it even harder for ourselves to hear Higher Self and all its empowering messages about how to actually get closer to our worth, our truth, and, most important, our purpose.

This I know because my job for nearly two decades was convincing consumers that they weren't enough so that my client could come to the rescue. Public relations is pretty self-explanatory. It is about helping a brand make itself relatable to the public so that brand can sell you something. The industry is built on the same system we've been talking about: the system of external as valuable, validation as reward, and fear or lack as the inherent truth within each of us, which is expertly leveraged to convince you that you need that brand.

In my time working in PR and marketing agencies, I did it all. I designed word-of-mouth campaigns to convince people to see the newest blockbuster movie, trained teams to infiltrate message boards and plant seeds about the newest cola flavor and how they just couldn't live without it. I led teams of creatives, data analysts, and messaging experts to understand exactly what an audience thought about, for example, driving, to help an oil and gas brand personalize itself to a younger audience.

I also got involved when a brand screwed up and hurt people or the environment. In those instances, my job became about trust. The question was: What can we do or say to help the public trust this leader or this brand again? Then we guided our clients to do it. Did we check in to make sure the brand meant those words? Maybe we liked to tell ourselves we had, but even we knew, working from behind our screens late into the night, writing press statements and devising damage control plans, that most of our clients just wanted words to say, in the sincerest tone they could muster, so they could get back to business as usual.

And it worked. Every time.

Are you ready to guess why? I bet by now you can. Because the system has trained us to believe external is better than internal.

Without the awareness of our inner wisdom, without being nurtured to believe we hold that deep knowing within, we look to the outside for the truth. That is the perfect conditioning for PR people like me (or who I used to be) to work with, because it means that when experts and leaders speak, others will listen, and at the end of the day, even if there's some cynicism, consumers will opt to believe that these experts know better somehow.

What excites me today is that this is changing. The agency I left years ago to do the work I do now spent years studying this trend, and our CEO would travel around the world telling brands that trust in them and their leaders was on the decline. The more social media grew, the more access consumers had to information about how products were developed, working conditions of employees, and the impact of commerce on our climate.

As information became more readily available to the average person, consumers began to see through the shiny PR and marketing campaigns and trust companies less. Consumers could check online reviews left by other customers before buying a product and employees had a platform to share the reality of their company's work culture. This has created real pressure on corporations, causing them to reluctantly provide more transparency into their operations, to meet the demand for honesty from their consumers.

That's movement in the right direction, sure, except that brands quickly figured out how to make themselves sound more like you. They hired new spokespeople, trained their employees to use social media to promote their brand, thus becoming cooler on social media, and still continuing to sell their stories betting on the fact that you still believe others more than you believe yourself.

This is how the business world has made your Higher Self the villain. Intuition is such an inner world, and consumer capitalism encourages us to live so externally and to accumulate things to show that we matter. The ads you see on Instagram are focused on the way you look, not the way you think and feel.

Personal success in a capitalist society is only about those external markers—cars and handbags and watches and the newest cream bronzer. We prioritize obtaining those markers over having peace of mind, a deep sense of fulfillment, or the ability to fully and totally live in the present without letting the hamster wheel of *what if*s and *shouldn't*s rob us of the moment.

The path to freedom from this "not enough" prison begins with redefining *fulfillment*. Check in with how much of the external world actually fulfills you. Yes, it may create a momentary high—for me too. No one loves an afternoon in Sephora more than me. But then what? Examine the aftermath. Do you really feel fulfilled from the $68 skin peel in the pretty pink bottle? Maybe for a minute, but not for long after that.

But you know where you do feel it? When you've done something that makes you feel genuinely connected to yourself and the world around you. Maybe it's going for a walk with a friend who needs an ear, or taking your kid for a surprise after-school ice cream cone, or blocking an hour on your calendar in the middle of the day to sit outside with your lunch and take in the fresh air.

No judgment here, by the way; everything has its place. Go buy those jeans you've wanted for weeks—that feels good too. I'm just asking that we remember there are deeper needs coming from within us. Our inner world needs connection and purpose to feel fully resourced. Think of it like a fuel tank that needs to be topped off. The jeans may add a few drops in, but then compare that to an afternoon spent with your best friend and see how much more that experience fills your tank. Freedom from this "buy this and you'll love yourself again" nonsense comes from becoming aware of what actually fills your inner tank instead of letting someone who's trying to sell you something define that for you.

For me lately, my fulfillment comes from connecting to the thing I value the most in life: freedom. I've learned not to judge the quality of my life by the designer clothes and bags I can afford or the famous clients whose numbers I have stored in my phone, but by the amount of free time in my day. That sweet feeling of flowing, spontaneously from one thing to another, following the call of my soul toward whatever it wants to experience. No system can give me that, which makes me wholly free of it. Pure, gorgeous defiance of something that wants so badly to control me.

### Structure 3: Education

A desire for conformity as a means for mass control is true no matter what system you look at: Did you know, for example, that our current education system was built to create obedience and efficiency in the population and prepare people for factory work over two hundred years ago? Before then, formal education was reserved for the elite, but with the rise of factories during the Industrial Revolution (1760 to 1840), the need for a uniform method of education to train workers and build a national identity, especially in the US, created our modern public schools. As Gerald Prokopowicz has written: "Educational reformers hoped to use public schools as a means to assimilate immigrants and achieve national unity by creating a uniform and universal educational experience."[2]

While our educational system has evolved past that, it is still a system that requires conformity to function. Conformity includes standardized tests and classroom hours spent sitting at a desk. This then creates an internal value of sitting in a room and being told about something over experiencing it firsthand. There's no greater block to creativity than that mode of operating.

Think back to your Higher Self when you first enter elementary school. All it wants you to do is go out there and experience! Then you show up in school and they tell you to sit down, be quiet, walk in a straight line, and mute all that splendid color inside into a gray that allows the system to flourish, not you. Another system that shuts down your truth, your Higher (intuitive) Self.

The most successful TED Talk of all time is about just this idea.[3] Sir Ken Robinson, an educator and speaker, came to speak to TED about how school is more like asking children to do hours of low-grade clerical work than it is about developing them as little, wonder-filled human beings ready to approach the world with curiosity and an open mind.

He described one girl being sent by her teachers to a doctor to be medicated for attention deficit hyperactivity disorder. The doctor refused. The girl, Gillian, didn't have ADHD; rather, she was a *dancer*. Regular school was not for her. She needed to be in an environment that celebrated her gifts, which her parents promptly found. She later graduated from the Royal Ballet School and went to work with Andrew Lloyd Webber choreographing his most famous musicals like *Cats* and *Phantom of the Opera*.

What if every child were met with this kind of open-mindedness rather than prescriptiveness? It's so difficult, because in school, independent thinking and action are not valued. Children are limited in how much they can advocate for themselves (Gillian the dancer was lucky to have someone who advocated for her). Because the education system gets us so young, from an early age we are not asked to check the information we are receiving against our own truth. This can be information about who we are, what are skills and abilities are, or even the world around us.

This gets dangerous if the education system we happen to be enrolled in is subject to certain cultural influences. Think about how some states are actively taking books out of schools or omitting certain topics related to history, racial justice, queer identity, and so on. Think about how this system relies on us not thinking for ourselves so we can accept the whitewashed version of facts as truth.

Among the books on the current banned list in Florida public schools are *The Handmaid's Tale*, *Their Eyes Were Watching God*, *And Tango Makes Three*, and *Forever*: respectively, a book about the dangerous effects on women's rights when religion enters politics, a story about a Black woman taking control of her own fate (and one of the most relevant books to Black culture), a picture book about two male penguins raising a chick, and a story written by beloved young adult author Judy Blume about female birth control.

What does that tell you about the direction our US education system is taking? What about the power of a system like this to define reality for growing minds? Whenever a system that is meant to educate you wants to control your thinking, it isn't trying to educate at all, it is attempting to dominate.

But what if, instead of dominate, the education system said: *Check in with yourself.* What if our schools encouraged children to explore their longings and desires?

One thing you can do to help make this vision of free and inclusive learning possible is to support organizations and after-school programs that encourage this form of learning and self-expression. I have the privilege of being on the board of a nonprofit called AHA!, a Santa Barbara–based organization that works hard to bring social/emotional intelligence back to the education system as a means to address the mental health crisis teenagers are facing in the US.

AHA! was founded by two mental health professionals, Dr. Jennifer Freed and Rendy Freedman, as a response to the Columbine shootings. They recognized in that travesty that teens need a safe space to express their emotions and feel seen and supported. Today, AHA! holds after-school groups in middle schools and high schools across the region, encouraging teens to show up, speak freely about their struggles, and learn to support each other in community and without shame.

This work is part of the vision I'm laying out here, but there are hundreds of other ways to support this vision. Help fund the arts in schools so kids can continue to express themselves freely. Volunteer for after-school programs that support the same. Even just staying vigilant about the ways our education system is robbing kids of their individuality and speaking up will make a difference. Awareness that it's happening and action from that place of awareness is all we need to create real change.

What saddens me most about this tightening of what we deem acceptable is that there are people living among us who have incredible gifts that come quite literally from their intuition, gifts that can change lives. They can sense future events. They can connect to people who have passed on to the other side. They can communicate with animals or the rest of nature in ways that some of us can't. They can look to our planets and stars and map out what's to come.

These people are secretly consulted. Police departments consult psychics on cold cases and CEOs work with astrologers to pick auspicious days for deals, but instead of these people and their gifts being publicly celebrated, we are trained to meet them with mockery and disbelief. You can be an accountant, but you can't be a medium—not if you want respect.

Once again, we are left to choose: Are we going to be respected for our intellect and reason, or are we going to be open to the gift of intuition as holding equal value? Most of us choose the former, while these awesomely talented, intuitive individuals end up villainized for their best gifts. We paint them as not being in their right mind. We decide there's something wrong with the way they think. That you're a fool if you open yourself up to their skills.

It's sad to think about all the childhood heroes we lost as we got older. The people we believed could talk to horses or predict the future or commune with the spirits. Age and education taught us to find them silly. But why can't science and intuition coexist? Nobel Prize–winning physicist Giorgio Parisi explains that oftentimes physicists would intuit a certain phenomenon, which would only be proven much later when science caught up with their hypothesis.[4] Niels Bohr, for example, speculated in 1913 that there was a simple way to calculate the "spectral lines of light" emitted by hydrogen. Classical physics had no ability to do this. Instead, a whole new field of science was required to validate his theory—quantum mechanics. Bohr had no evidence to support his theory, but he felt intuitively it was right.

What if we could just accept that all thought starts with inner wisdom and branches out from there? If we didn't accept that all wisdom needed to be incepted into us by the education system or the media? What could we learn about ourselves? What could we come to accept about the world? There's a reason we think inventors and our greatest luminaries are crazy before the rest of the world eventually catches up to them. What if instead we celebrated the full extent of their gifts as they were creating?

Remember that teenage you? The one who had to reconnect to Higher Self to express their individuality? What if, in those high school classrooms, you were encouraged to turn the flame up on that dialogue? What if you were taught that you were intuitive then? What would you have done differently?

We are always learning, so it's never too late to incorporate our intuitive knowing with what we're being taught. As you expand, work on differentiating between learning and knowing. You will have to juggle both. *Learning* is defined in Webster's dictionary as "gaining knowledge or understanding of or skill by study, instruction, or experience." *Knowing*, on the other hand, is defined as "perceiving something directly and recognizing the nature of that thing."

Do you see where your intuitive voice lives? It's in the recognition space. Use your intuitive wisdom to check the things you're learning against your knowing. Which part of you recognizes what you're learning and which part does not? Which part of you is asking you to go deeper or find a new angle? And are the things you're learning allowing you to expand?

Much like the work around questioning the common narrative delivered by media, know that education should feel like an expansion, not a contraction. If you're learning something or the process through which you're being taught something feels like shame or creates a contracted feeling within, that thing is not for you. Your knowing will allow you to accept or reject what doesn't truly sere your best interest. .

For example, if you read a book that speaks to a certain part of your own truth, but someone tells you that book is bad or wrong, instead of feeling shame about your connection to it, honor the part of you that felt recognition in those pages and discard the external opinion as projection, not reality.

I share a lot in common with our eldest son, my stepson Keegan. He's deeply intuitive and emotionally intelligent. He's also a talented musician, which I am unequivocally not. But we are also both easily distracted. He's not diagnosed with any particular label, but in me it shows up as ADHD. Recently, Keegan was writing a paper for his English class about the negative effects of media on young girls. He lives with his mother in the Bay Area, and so one night we were on FaceTime, and he was telling his dad and me that he had this paper to write as he strummed his guitar, feeling guilty about not getting it done.

"What did you like about the documentary you watched on media?" I asked him.

"That it's sad that girls get so many messages about how they're supposed to be. I don't think I knew that," he said.

"Sounds like you have your first paragraph right there," I told him. "Why don't you play me a song, then write that down, and then play me another song?"

An hour and four songs later, Keegan had his paper written.

"That was fun!" he said, as we were saying good night.

A teenage boy called the writing of an essay fun! Why? Because we gave him permission to check what he was learning against his knowing self. To stop, strum, move his body, let the learning settle into his being, and then reflect. By being reminded of his own intuitive way of being as an asset in his learning, not a liability, he was able to see himself as not only capable of writing, but also to discover that he was actually quite good at articulating himself in this way.

How can you do that as you learn new things? How can you incorporate your whole being into what you're learning? How can you change the process to meet you where you're at instead of falling short in a system that was never designed for you to begin with? Keegan's story is about doing that in the smallest way and still feeling represented in the process. What does that light up for you?

*Structure 4: Culture*

Growing up, I *loved* TV (still do). As a latchkey kid, I watched sitcoms voraciously not only to deal with my boredom and loneliness, but also because I really do love a good comedic misunderstanding and the shenanigans that ensue. I watched reruns of *Three's Company*, *I Love Lucy*, *Good Times*, *The Golden Girls*, *The Jeffersons*, *Who's the Boss?*, *The Cosby Show*, and, as I got older, *Saved by the Bell* and *Beverly Hills 90210* (okay, that one's not so funny, but you get the point).

I literally think I watched them all—and anything else that was made between the 1950s and the 1990s. What did I see there? I saw *mostly* white people. I saw nuclear families where the mom and dad were married, and the kids lived under one roof. I saw privilege, even if it was just the TV family going out for a meal that my family couldn't afford. (I do think this is why *Good Times* was one of my favorites; it made me feel more at home than the rest.) Regardless, you know who I never saw in these shows? Myself.

My parents were divorced, and kids constantly asked me where I was born (they were even more confused when I'd say New Mexico). Meanwhile, on television, the images I saw told me that "good" looked like being white, "success" looked like having a family that stayed together, and "worth" looked like having the means to afford anything you wanted. While loving what I was watching and being entertained, I also had a growing belief in me that I was in fact not enough. So, I straightened my hair. I learned how to talk as "white" as I could. I made friends with mostly white kids. I hid the Persian lunch my grandmother packed me.

I assimilated, and if I'm being honest, in some ways I still do. It's built into me, this desire for assimilation. It feeds the limiting belief that I'm not enough as I am. It feeds many of our limiting beliefs about what being enough looks like. It weaves stories about gender that are limiting, about race that are limiting, about class and socioeconomic status that are limiting. We watch these culture-making shows and movies and we decide that if those things are normal, beautiful, or good, the parts of us that don't match are abnormal, ugly, or bad. Everyone makes those decisions, and because they make them about themselves, they feel emboldened to make them about others.

It's from this place that we shame and judge and insult others. This place of deep internal shame says, *You're not good enough.* When that shame within us sees what flashes across the screen, in the pages of a fashion magazine, or on a TikTok, it gets louder.

*See,* it says, *I told you you're not good enough. Just look at that. You'll never be that good. But keep trying. That's the only way to make me go away.*

That voice is a lot to bear. To release the pressure, we take that inner voice and make it our outer voice. We look at people who challenge the culture norms and decide they are dangerous. Remember those hate posts littering Alok's social media? That's a perfect example of this dynamic at play.

*How dare they not give into this pressure,* shame says.

We're angry at them because we want the freedom they have. So, we hurl our shame in fits of rage toward others instead of looking at the shame itself. What does it really want?

What it is craving is the freedom that those who go against the culture have in expressing their truth. If I got to externally express myself in a way that brought me the most joy, what would I be doing? What would I wear? What would I say? Answer those questions for yourself. Recognizing that you don't do, say, or wear those things because of the fear of not fitting into what the culture has defined is an awakening you won't forget.

My favorite quote, which is commonly attributed to the poet Anaïs Nin but is actually from a 1979 poem by Elizabeth Appell, reads: "And the day came when the risk to remain tight in a bud was more painful than the risk it took to blossom."[5] I promise you that you'll hear it again in this book. I'll refer to it over and over on this journey to liberate you because it encapsulates in those twenty-three words exactly what it is to choose your expanded self over shrinking to meet the world's demands.

When it comes down to a choice between fitting in or living your truth, the time will come where the cost of fitting in will get too high and the reward of living your truth too tempting. When that day comes you will go from following the culture set for you to becoming the culture maker. If we want a world that values love over hate, then we need culture makers that come from truth. We need culture makers that are aligned with their expanded selves. We need our culture makers to create culture from their highest frequency instead of their shame-filled shadow self. We need this so that we may all rise, collectively, to the highest frequency within us.

### If You Believe It, Then It's True

If you believe it, then it's true, my teacher Ms. Penn said.

Now I know what she was also saying is that belief, when it's solely driven from the outside, is dangerous. We have been trained for centuries to believe things because other people tell us to. We believe what our teachers, parents, elected officials, celebrity influencers—whoever we value—tell us what to believe in. They tell us what success looks like, what good looks like, what beauty looks like. They tell us what dreams to strive for and which ones are out of our reach. Everything has become externally validated, even our beliefs.

Relying on others to define our beliefs is creating a chasm within us, and Higher Self becomes the casualty. The more we listen to external voices, the less we tune into our own, internal voice. We've created a zero-sum game, believing that if we need others to define our reality and make us feel valued then we can't fulfill those needs from within, alone, without help.

Mass control to motivate behavior is never good when it's motivated by shame—the process is bad, or the end point is bad. Remember that our Higher Selves are there to help us thrive, which means that *all* of us must thrive. Our inner wisdom isn't the one creating separation, it's our fear and our anxiety doing that. By learning to trust our own Higher Self, we allow others to try and tap in and listen to theirs, which is where they will find empathy and love for themselves and for others.

But when we're stuck with this trade-off mindset, what happens to that wise voice from within? To our Higher Self? It just continues to fade into the background, watching as we construct our lives not from a place of its, and our own, inner wisdom and power, but in the image of what's being projected by others and by the commonly accepted standards.

It watches as we construct our perfect tidy little boxes, each in the same size and shape as the other (even though we like to believe that painting them different colors makes us original).

It watches as we lose ourselves in what we *should* want to help quiet the shame voice.

It watches as we wake up each morning, on autopilot, continuing to pursue what others tell us to, and look to them to tell us we're doing a good job while we're doing it.

It watches patiently, knowing that a tornado built of all this inauthentic action is brewing inside.

It feeds the tornado, filling us with a longing we can't quite describe.

It whispers and whispers until soon the life we built, in the image of others, feels like it is suffocating us.

It waits there, right behind the breakdown, for its invitation to reemerge in its fullest glory.

EXPLORATION: *Testing the Systems*

Let's take a minute now and figure out how some of these systems may have contributed to your own disconnect from your Higher Self. Try, as best you can, to refrain from judgment. I want to remind you that this work is about self-awareness, not blame, of yourself or anyone else.

Ready? Answer the questions below and take as much time to really detail your thoughts. The goal is to reach for as much awareness as possible, to turn on those light bulbs within and in doing so, reattach the parts of you that have been disconnected from your power, your Higher Self.

- Pick two or three of the systems from this chapter (media, capitalism, education or culture) that you grew up in that defined things like "good," "success," "beauty," "worth" for you.
- Now, next to each, list all the ways these systems influenced how you saw yourself. For example: *I was an artist who learned better through hands-on experience but was taught that I was unintelligent because I didn't succeed at memorizing a textbook or taking tests.* Get really specific with these statements.
- Read back through your list once you're done. Next to each statement, write a few words about how these beliefs still live in you now. For example: *I still sometimes feel like I'm not as intellectual as others and usually feel this way when I hear people talking about the latest novel they've read.*
- Finally, for each, write out how you can reframe this belief by seeing your own unique gifts as superpowers. For example: *I'm able to see color and light in a way few people do and because of that, I make art that helps people actually stop and feel their feelings in an increasingly disconnected world.*

CHAPTER 6

# Anything for Love

*P*rimed with the limiting beliefs implanted by our environment, romantic relationships become the fastest way we lose ourselves. Here's the simple reason why: When we first fall in love, it's not exactly with another person. What we *really* fall in love with is the way someone makes us feel about ourselves. Yes, we may admire or desire certain aspects of the other person immediately but loving them for who they are takes so much longer, because you don't immediately "know" another person. So, no, that intense feeling that hits us in the beginning is not love for another; it is love for the way they make us feel about ourselves, and the possibility for how they could love us.

In truth, when someone falls in love with us, they conjure a version of our Higher Selves for us to behold, and Higher Self being as magnificent as it is, we fall in love at first sight with it. Not knowing that Higher Self is available to us all the time, that it's a part of us, that we're the ones who can easily conjure it, we attribute this experience to the person who is making us feel this way. It's addictive, this feeling, but again, we don't know yet that we don't need anyone else to find and embody our highest frequency, so we get addicted to this other person. We feel we need them to be whole. That without them, we will shrivel, contract, go back to the dark place they pulled us from.

This is where the problems come in. If the other person is not operating from their Higher Self, if instead they are still in their shame body, we are attaching ourselves to a sinking ship. I know, dramatic. But it's true. Finding love in unhealed spaces is . . . I want to say impossible, but instead I'll say rare. This is especially true in our twenties and thirties. I should know. I got married, for the first time, at twenty-five, at my own insistence. My ex-husband didn't want to get married so young.

"I don't know myself yet," he'd say anytime I brought it up.

I couldn't accept that. I had a plan: married by twenty-five, first kid by twenty-eight and second by thirty. He was either going to fit into my plan or I would move on. That was my ultimatum.

Why? I needed him to make me feel whole, to feel less afraid of re-creating my mom's journey of a single-parent household. I never had a nuclear family like the ones I saw on TV; he was my chance at fixing that. I felt like the more emotional care he needed from me, the better. Remember, I had been trained from an early age to take on and heal other people's difficult feelings—his need for healing fit my superpower perfectly. I'd fix him right up and then I'd have the picture-perfect family I'd always wanted. Win-win.

He was more intuitive in the beginning than I was. He knew, from his Higher Self, that marriage at that age would be disastrous for him—and for me—but what do you do when the person you love and feel safest with uses that intimacy to force your hand? You give in.

And he did: we were married at twenty-five, first kid by twenty-eight and the second by thirty. I got my way. Everything was perfect. Except that by twenty-nine, the fighting got so bad I cried at least twice a week and by thirty-one, I was separated. Now the picturesque family I had created was meeting in a gas station parking lot to hand off toddlers and their toys.

Has he forgiven me for forcing him away from his Higher Self's wise advice? My hope is that every time he looks at our two kids, he finds a way to, but deep down, I know there's a part of him that wishes he had listened to his intuitive wisdom over his desire to satisfy me. I give him that. I never regret a single thing about my first marriage, especially because I ended up with two incredible humans as kids, but I do wish I had honored his pace, instead of insisting on action based on my own gaping, terrified wounds.

We have all mistaken relationships for shelter. We walk this long road of self-doubt and isolation as we navigate our growth and our distance from our Higher Self. Then, we come upon a person who seems to somehow see that glimmer of our inner magic, even though we've lost sight of it ourselves. It feels like they hold the lighter to that flame, and we see in them a return to something we can faintly remember from our freer, childhood days. Of course, we don't have the words or the consciousness to name it; we just feel it, and that feeling is addictive.

The spark we feel when we think of that person, the way they make us feel just by looking in our direction, that feeling is like a drug. We attribute all this bubbliness to the other person. We forget that it's just a reflection of what's buried deep within. We can't get enough of them, and we can't live without them. After all those years of learning how to seek validation by distancing ourselves from our truth, we come armed with the most effective strategy to hold on to this feeling, to this person: we know we can become whoever they want to keep them in our lives, and so, we do.

The tragedy of this is that love is all about self-actualization. Love, romantic or otherwise, is the highest expansion of ourselves. Love that sees and celebrates your true essence is one of the most important aids you will have in your journey to reconnect with Higher Self. People who love you truly can sometimes see the higher aspects of yourself before you can.

That said, our endless search for romantic love, the desire for which is trained into us from a young age, is not necessarily the same thing as soul-expanding love. When we should be looking for the latter, we obsess over the former. Why? There are three main reasons this happens: our training, our ideas about love, and the way we intermingle our attachments with our identity.

### How Our Training Teaches Us to Prioritize Marriage

Remember all the seeds that have been implanted along the way by our family, culture, media, and friends? That training paints a pretty picture that most definitely includes a monogamous, state-sanctioned relationship that lasts a lifetime. That training tells us there is one soulmate for each of us, leading us to believe that when we find them, we better never lose them. Losing your one soulmate—is there a bigger failure than that? Our training teaches us to seek this person in everything we do, and it also teaches us that we must do what it takes to keep them.

Cultural training around relationships is the most indoctrinating type. In my highly patriarchal Persian culture, for instance, young women are taught that getting a husband is the greatest triumph we can hope for and that keeping a husband is the only pathway to demonstrate our value. Even though I was born in the US, that training was profoundly a part of who I used to be. That training created the ultimatum I gave my ex; I had to be married to be valuable.

This kind of thinking is true of many, many cultures, and it has been this way for centuries. This training is deep in our history. Our romantic ideas about marriage and partnership were formed from a completely utilitarian and economic need. It wasn't until 1974 when the Equal Credit Opportunity Act granted women the right to open a bank account on their own. That means that for most of our history, women have needed men to have any financial security whatsoever. As a result, they were seen as financial burdens to their families. The only way to handle this liability was to marry them off and make them some other man's financial responsibility.

Even if you were a young woman who came from great wealth, that wealth was rarely ever yours. You would become a pawn in a business or political deal that secured your family greater power, more land, or additional influence. Marriage is a trade deal; that's its origin. We've been trained to believe it's necessary to make us whole as humans when, in truth, it was only ever created as a tool to manage economics. For most of history, we were at least more honest about the reality of marriage. Now, we expect our partners to be half of an economic relationship while also being our romantic partners *and* best friends.

This economic arrangement isn't a history lesson. It is alive and well today. Can you think of someone who is in a relationship for the financial security? Maybe that someone is you. There's no judgment in that. I have close, dear friends who are married with children and stay because of their finances. It's not an easy situation to navigate, especially when they've chosen to give up their financial freedom for the good of the family or the relationship.

You'll never catch me telling these friends that what they've chosen is wrong. It's a choice they've made from their training. That's not the important part. What's important is that when that choice is made, there's honesty about what's being given. Is it possible to exist in a relationship like this and still be in touch with your truth? Absolutely! But it's not easy.

A client of mine talks to me about her sister in our sessions. They grew up in an upper-middle-class neighborhood, everyone craning their neck to see who had what and to keep up with each other. Their parents both worked, so the model was there to set them both up as women who made their own living, pursuing their own passions and careers. Her sister was brilliant, graduated with a degree from a well-regarded university, got a great job in finance out of college, and was on her way to building a career of her own. Except there was one thing.

Somewhere along the way, even with two working parents, something in her training told her the perfect life meant she would marry a successful man and be a stay-at-home mom. Is there something inherently wrong with this choice? Absolutely not. Spending your time with your children, being there to guide and navigate when they need you most, is a grueling job that no salary could ever reward. But the trouble for her began when she chose her partner not for their deep connection or his ability to build her up and see her truth, but from the reality that he could fit this financial picture perfectly.

My client will often get emotional in our sessions as she tells me about her brother-in-law and the way he treats her sister now that they have four kids. He reminds her often that she doesn't contribute financially, which is why he shouldn't help out with the kids or the house. He disregards her ideas, belittles her feelings, all the while reminding her that this lifestyle was her choice. It's devastating for my client to watch her incredibly intelligent, capable sister reduced to tears by a man who not only doesn't see her magic but also works actively to make sure she forgets it too. She's forgotten her truth to fit into this relationship, because the financial need dictated the terms. This outcome is only possible because of her training.

My training told me to make similar sacrifices in my first marriage. My training taught me to rush past the dating phase and insist on marriage because twenty-five was approaching. It was my training that said it wasn't about the depth of our spiritual connection but about following a predetermined road map. My training forced an ultimatum on a man who was working hard against his own training to follow his gut. Look at where that took us.

### Love as External

Don't worry—I'm not so cynical that I believe training is the only reason we commit to or seek partnership. Love is of course a monumental force that drives us toward entanglement with another. We can experience genuine love for another, so profound that with them we are better. We can't see our lives without their loving presence. It's a real feeling. It's what makes life so rich and exciting and meaningful. We are nothing without love.

And yet, the second reason we lose ourselves in relationships is based on a limiting belief we have about love: we believe that love is an external condition.

When we are shown love, we believe love is an external thing being given to us, that being given love on the outside means we are worthy of it on the inside. Not only have we been taught that we need to experience external love to have it at all, we've also been taught that love in its greatest form exists only in romantic relationships. We believe that the only way to experience this magical feeling is through a romantic relationship. This myth makes us chase love by hook or by crook. We are willing to sacrifice our truth by making decisions that sabotage our ability to live a life that reflects who we really are, what we truly want, and ultimately, our purpose here.

But love is an energy that is just so much bigger than all that. When we condense love to something that can only happen between two people, we miss the point. Love is the only thing in the entire universe that is true. Love is the energy from which we came. It's the energy that made every single thing we see. Love is creation.

Even the things that harm us are related to love. Fear, hatred, violence—all of those things are just love disfigured. The material of love is still present within them, it's just been twisted, poked through, thinned out, and sometimes washed away. Love is all there is. We are love, which means we cannot actually be *without* love. We don't require it from anyone for it to be true. Our very existence makes it true. That inner whisper, the fire that burns inside us, *that* is love. Turning our loving gaze inward at that sacred fire can show us that we are full of endless love. We are here to give love. Yes, receiving it is important if not vital, but it isn't our only chance at love. It is simply one tiny sliver.

When we stop confusing external love as the only source of love, whether this is something we receive or believe we are here to give to others, we create infinite possibility for love within our own lives. It's only when we see and love the fire burning within that we magnetize that same energy into our lives. Then we can give and receive love from a place of truth instead of trying to fill a hole that can never be filled from the outside.

To say it more plainly, loving ourselves is the only way we can truly accept love from others. Without that foundation, we don't actually believe we are worthy of love and no amount of love coming to us will feel like enough.

### Attachment and Our Identity

I have a close friend who hates meeting their friends' partners. We laugh about it, but when I ask them to explain, they say that it's hard for them to sit through lunch or dinner watching who they knew their friends to be turn into someone else in the presence of their partners.

The first time I heard them articulate it that way, I had to stop and think. *They're right.*

Our training and our definition of love as external have so much to do with why we alter our behaviors within a relationship. It makes sense, of course; we believe that romantic relationships define our value, so we become what the other person wants or needs in order to stay together. But I also find that our identities become entangled with our relationship status. "Wife," "husband," "partner." We take these titles seriously when instead it's the commitments they represent that we mean to take seriously. A commitment is not the same as an identity. When we confuse the two, we lose sight of ourselves.

What if your Higher Self whispers things to you that you don't put in the same category as one of those labels? Identity crisis! I see it all the time.

"I'm a married man with two kids," a client recently told me when we achieved the realization together that he wants to leave his job as CEO to pursue his passion for travel photography.

The couple had more than enough savings to make this happen, not to mention his husband had an incredibly high-earning job.

"What does one have to do with the other?" I asked. "More

important," I wondered, "have you thought about talking to your husband about this desire? Are you sure he'd be that rocked by it?"

He did talk to him, eventually, and of course his partner was not surprised. He was, in fact, relieved. Often our partners can see the truths we try to bury deep; they see us become less of ourselves as we ignore our truth. If they really love us, all they want is for us to admit this truth to ourselves and start chasing the inner fire. They want to see us come to life in this more authentic way. But the attachment to this identity as husband and father told my client a different story. It said, *This is the entirety of who you are, plus the CEO part. There is no room for anything else.*

We become attached to these identities: the person we think we need to be to keep the relationship plus the label we've given ourselves in the relationship. The problem is we are ever-changing beings. We grow and expand—that's the whole point. Our job here is to keep growing and growing until we can't grow anymore. Can you see how attaching to an identity you created at any point in your life to secure a relationship gets in the way of this expansion?

This attachment to our identity in the relationship creates major fear of Higher Self. We know it's in there, whispering to us constantly, and we also know that it may whisper truths that will make us have to change from the person we promised to be. I often think that's where the concept of midlife crisis comes from. It is not so much the midlife part that's relevant; it's that people grow out of who they promised other people they would be. This growth is highly inconvenient to others in their lives, so they describe it as a crisis.

What if instead we went into relationships knowing that change is the only constant in life? What if instead of promising to remain exactly the same forever, we promised to keep listening to the voice that wants us to expand? What if we promised the people we loved that we would facilitate this process for them? My husband and I made these vows to each other when we got married. We didn't promise to love, honor, and cherish through sickness and health. We promised to always see the other person's Higher Self and to act as a flashlight when one of us lost sight of our own truth. We promised to push each other to grow and expand, even if that sends us in different directions, because that is what love is.

Love is growth. Love between two people is about facilitating that growth. When we're unconscious of that reality, we facilitate that growth by hurting each other. When we're conscious, we facilitate that growth through self-exploration and courageous conversations. We do it without fear of loss. If we really love another, what we want more than anything is for the other person to live their truth, not hide it for our benefit.

Real, sustainable love means wanting ourselves and our partners to fully embody their truth. Love is liberation. The way I see it, our society is geared against people who operate from a mindset that isn't the norm—aka a monogamous commitment between a man and a woman.

I have learned most of what I know as a coach about love from my queer clients. I have watched them learn to love what is inside first. I have watched them learn to honor their truth above all else. I have watched them value their relationship with Higher Self so much they refuse to trade it in for acceptance. They had to. They exist in a world that says they shouldn't exist. The only way to survive that profound rejection of your truth is to learn to love it fiercely.

Maybe, if we could all learn that love is internal, that it is wild and free and available endlessly to each of us, we can stop trying to keep it from each other. We can stop guarding it like Gollum and his gold ring, until we become so twisted and disfigured with our role as guardians of love that we push away the very thing we need most.

*You can have both.*

Your relationship is not the end of your journey toward Higher Self; your relationship is here to facilitate that journey. Your partner can be your guide, either by reflecting your Higher Self to you so that even when it's lost to you, you can be reminded of your inherent glory, or by missing your Higher Self altogether, reminding you of how bad it feels to be separated from this version of yourself and teaching you to choose your Higher Self over this person.

No, it doesn't mean that you need to leave your relationship to make this happen. It's not a binary. There is a lot in between. You can have both, but you have to be willing to confront all the blocks that tell you differently. You have to examine your training, your need for love from the outside, and the way you define your identity when in a relationship.

This is an exploration your Higher Self is waiting to lead you through. It may have even been whispering to you the whole time you've been reading this chapter. What is it saying that you're afraid to hear? What if I were to tell you that it's okay to listen? That just listening to hear what it has to say is enough right now. That you don't have to do anything with the information you get.

If you're in a relationship that doesn't allow you to be who you are or requires you to perform a version of yourself that is designed to make the other person comfortable, Higher Self will begin to pull you out of this performance and back to yourself. But know this: whatever that change is, whether it's more honesty with your current partner that transforms your relationship or channeling the courage you need to move on, either way it is leading you to that real love. When you get there, it is ecstasy.

Healed love is an experience that is so fortifying and fulfilling that, once you have it, you won't recognize the you that accepted anything less. You'll know you have it when the most honest, realest part of you gets to exist freely and is met by encouragement and tenderness. When you make decisions for yourself knowing that your partner will honor what's in your highest good because even if it's inconvenient or uncomfortable for them, what's best for you *is* what's best for the union you've created together.

That's what Higher Self wants for you—to heal those broken pieces within through your relationship with it, not by searching for someone else to do it for you. From that healed space, you raise your energetic frequency and arrive at an entirely new elevation, where you will recognize others who have done the same work.

Here, you will find partners who aren't looking to you to complete them, but rather are whole in themselves, allowing you to continue to grow and expand exactly as your soul desires, while they do the same alongside you. Being loved in this way only moves you more into alignment with Higher Self. You will begin to see that in this love, partnership comes only by following your truth, desires, and deep inner wisdom. That is love—to love ourselves and our beloveds so completely we don't seek to possess, but to liberate them into their truth and thus, their highest frequency.

This might sound frightening to some of you. Our training has taught us that love is possession, that freedom and love are oxymorons. We have limiting beliefs that tell us that granting freedom to our partners means they will no longer choose us. Do you see the folly in that? Believing that we have the right to stand in the way of our beloved's expansion into Higher Self just so we can remain loved and safe? This is a trade-off none of us should be asked to make.

Yet, some of us have been trained to fear our partner's freedom of self-discovery. We've been trained to fear that this journey will take them away from us. Motivated by that limiting belief, by that aching fear, we decided we will instead hold them as our prisoners based on commitments they made at a different stage of their soul's expansion.

This is how we end up stuck, unhappy, unfulfilled, and disconnected from our Higher Selves. We force commitment to be something that requires our partners to promise to never change and, therefore, we believe the call from Higher Self toward our own expansion is dangerous, and we ignore it. This is how our relationships distance us from our highest truth. But when we find love from this healed space, love that makes room for our expansion, it can be the greatest catalyst toward aligning with Higher Self there is.

I promise you not because it's convenient to, but because I took the same terrifying leap. Yes, in my case, it did lead me away from my first marriage. I won't lie to you—it was painful. But that pain is the very thing that led me fully back to my Higher Self... eventually.

EXPLORATION: *Relationship Deep Dive*

In this exercise you have the chance to uncover how your limiting beliefs have influenced your romantic life and to create something new that is aligned to your Higher Self. Use the following prompts to explore and rebuild:

1. What are some limiting beliefs that you've held that have influenced the way you see romantic love? How have other people's relationships (could be your parents' or anyone else's) influenced your limiting beliefs?
2. What do you believe being in a relationship says about you?
3. If your answers to the second question were positive, is it true that you have to be in a relationship for the above to be true? If so, why?
4. If romantic love was only a path toward living completely as your Higher Self:
   - *What would it feel like to be in that relationship?*
   - *What would your partner be like?*
   - *What would become possible for you that doesn't feel possible today?*

CHAPTER 7

# Hitting the Wall

I *was twenty-six when my grandmother* died, and I came home from the tiny service we held for her at my mom's house to find my husband passed out on our couch. He'd forgotten about the service because he'd been out drinking with a friend.

*He'll grow out of it*, I told myself, for the tenth time that year.

I knew something was wrong, but I ignored it because I wanted, so badly, to be married. And, well, our honeymoon period felt like anything but. Just a year after the wedding I received a call from the state police: "Your husband has rolled his car. He's in the emergency room."

It was after midnight when I drove to the hospital, shaking with fear. My driving was so wobbly that I actually got pulled over by the very same police officer who had found my husband on the side of the highway. The officer took one look at my shaking hands on the steering wheel and thought I was drunk driving too. *The irony*. My husband got seventy staples in his scalp that night. As we looked through the photos of his gnarled Toyota Scion, he'd promised, with fear coursing through his veins, to never drink again.

A year passed. One night, when our firstborn was six months old, my husband didn't come home after a night out. Panicked, I went outside in the hopes of seeing his headlights heading home only to find him asleep in the neighbor's yard.

At twenty-eight, I found out that another baby was on the way. My marriage had escalated into a predictable and exhausting cycle: something terrible would happen that would make him frightened by the drinking, which would drive him to promises of sobriety, which eventually would send us back to *start* because of "one innocent drink" with dinner. Meanwhile, we were trying to raise a toddler and keep our marriage afloat.

During our vows, it seemed that I had made an unspoken agreement in this marriage: I was the one that would hold it together, smiling in front of friends and family to hide my embarrassment during drunken outbursts, turning the other cheek when the alcohol took his anger from tolerable to frightening, and getting up to go to work to give the 200 percent it required to be the breadwinner I had to be.

For years it was like this. I was an educated, successful woman with an incredibly supportive and loving family who always had my back. How did I allow my own life to come off the rails at the hands of someone else?

*Deep down I knew something was wrong, but I ignored it.*

Why?

I did it because of what I believed. More specifically, because of what my own limiting belief systems caused me to believe.

As the youngest child of divorced parents, I believed a traditional nuclear family was the only path to security. As a confused and misunderstood Iranian American girl who never fit in, I believed that just being loved by someone, *anyone* was enough. As a child who did not grow up with her father around, I believed that a man's attention was the ultimate reward no matter what it took.

It was all the limiting beliefs coming together to cause me to create a life I thought I should want. My childhood pains, the influence of outside systems on my ideas of happiness and success—all of it mixed together and told me this was the life I was supposed to want.

Things came to a head when my beliefs began to be challenged by another voice. Beyond my facade of silent tolerance, there was a storm brewing inside me, a battle between two powerful forces: my Higher Self and my limiting belief systems. My Higher Self, the gentle warrior, was beginning to force her way through, confidently whispering that there was more out there than a life that was so hard, so filled with pain.

She'd make it difficult to ignore the long nights of drunken fights, keeping me awake with simple thoughts like *You don't have to live this way.* She'd force my voice to break through the contraction in my throat, fighting my fear voice—telling me not to start another argument on a Sunday afternoon or risk losing his love right before my birthday—with the newer idea, *Love earned by staying silent isn't love at all.*

Her whispers began quietly but gained strength. Higher Self was constantly telling me that my silence wasn't my truth, that I had more to say—much, much more. She was bold. She was large and she hated, absolutely hated, how much we had shrunk to fit into this marriage, this life. She wanted more and she was beginning to get tired of being pushed into the recesses of my mind, of being told she wasn't real, that she was as imaginary as a fairy tale. She grew powerful, channeling her guidance to me through the only language she knew: my intuition.

But the fear loomed large over everything else. Every time I decided to stand up for myself, it would push its way through, stand in the spotlight, and shout louder and more clearly: *DO NOT LISTEN TO THAT IMAGINARY VOICE.* My fear voice had developed over my entire lifetime to try and protect me. It interpreted every difficult experience as evidence that its protection was necessary to our survival. In this marriage it was pleading: *To be secure we need to be in a family . . . don't screw that up for us.*

Despite the power of that fear, my Higher Self never let up. She would show up in my quiet moments, in my dreams, in my moments of pain, always with the same loving, gentle, but powerful message: *There is more for you in this life, and I assure you, you will have it.* She didn't care that I ignored her. She didn't care that I was frightened of her message. She just kept showing up. She knew that one day, when I remembered her and how real she was, I would finally listen.

That moment finally came at twenty-nine. I was eight months pregnant with my son when I found myself sitting on the kitchen floor sobbing amid yet another argument with my husband as he hurled insults at me before going into the backyard. I sat on the floor, unable to get up. I was wailing, gushing out grief and hurt onto the kitchen floor, when my husband walked back inside. He walked right past me, then stopped, looked at me, shook his head in disgust, and kept on walking, leaving me there to finish my breakdown and claw at the cabinet doors to help me stand when I was done.

BAM.

It was like something inside me broke open. Seeing him walk away from my pain was all it took to let Higher Self finally break through, shattering the glass wall I had put between me and it.

*It's time to go*, she said. *It won't be easy, but it will be worth it.*

I had my son, and eighteen months later, I separated from my husband.

### The Phoenix Process

Those eighteen months were a master class in learning how to reunite with my Higher Self. Moments of fear were woven with moments of intuitive clarity.

See, just because my Higher Self finally broke through with clear guidance doesn't mean my fear voice let her win right away. I'd take four steps forward—four steps toward my freedom—and then five steps back. I was engaged in a dance between my Higher Self and every one of my limiting beliefs. I'd start speaking up more, taking more space when I needed it, spending more time with friends, or taking trips to visit my family in North Carolina without him and I'd begin to see the possibility of a life without him forming.

The minute that vision would become clear to me, my fear

fought back, reminding me what that vision really meant: weekends without my babies, a cold, lonely bed at night, becoming the very same single mom I watched struggle when I was young.

Some days I'd decide fear was right, and plaster the smile back on my face, concede, stay quiet, distract myself from the things I didn't want to see. But slowly, as my life crumbled around me, Higher Self began to feel less like an enemy to fight or a nuisance to ignore and more like a dance partner, at first moving awkwardly but then together with me in a graceful rhythm. My remembering who she was and starting to listen to her again made her louder, more decisive, and powerful.

I was in my **phoenix process.** I first heard that term shortly after my divorce when I read the incredible memoir by Elizabeth Lesser about her own divorce and self-actualization, *Broken Open*. The phoenix process in our journey is a life-altering, magical, painful, earth-shattering event or moment where everything we knew to be real or who we believed we were burns down to the ground so that another, more powerful self can emerge.

I really do love this mythology because it's the perfect allegory for reawakening to your Higher Self. The phoenix is an ancient symbol of rebirth. In Egyptian mythology, the phoenix was said to be as large as an eagle with stunning gold and scarlet feathers and a melodic caw. The phoenix existed alone as the only one of its kind. It lived this way for five hundred years. As the end of its life approached, the phoenix created its own funeral pyre out of spices and tree boughs and set itself on fire. Consumed in the flames, the phoenix disappeared into ash, but from the pyre, miraculously, a new phoenix emerged.

Connecting with your Higher Self is exactly that moment. This phoenixing is the opening our Higher Self has been waiting so patiently for. As you grow and forget your old friend, continuously trading in its loving and devoted guidance for the opinions of others, your Higher Self sits unbothered, knowing that this day will come. The day where the set you built around yourself out of painted cardboard begins to change from reality to empty fiction.

The day when you look around and see that the things you were supposed to want are not true to who you are deep down. This yearning calling from within, the one that says, *There's more out there*, this is your Higher Self calling to you to come find it again. To join it in once again discovering who you are. Once you hear it, you can't unhear it.

You are here, on Earth, to know yourself. To get to where you are now, you had to spend some time lost in the symphony of pressures and ideals that swirled around you. It's as if you've been working through a pile of jackets, trying each one on, looking for the perfect fit. Sometimes you even found one that felt like it fit perfectly, like it was exactly who you are. But then, as soon as it grew comfortable, you outgrew it. That too is part of the journey. The question you're trying to answer is a big one: *Who am I really?*

It is okay not to know. Remember that you've been trained from a very early age not to know yourself fully. You've been trained to be more interested in other people's answer to that question than your own. This is why the phoenix process is such a valuable part of your spiritual journey: it reawakens you to *your soul's longings*. Arriving at this reawakening can hurt. Watching the things you strived for and grew attached to begin to fall apart can be crushing.

And yet, it's in those dark, devastating transformations that you get to decide who you want to be.

Transformation is such a natural part of life here on Earth and yet we fight it with everything we have. We watch tree leaves turn orange and red in glorious fall landscapes, and we watch them fall to the ground as autumn turns to winter. We hold little caterpillars in our hands as kids and awe at the cocoons we see them build, emerging as brightly painted butterflies. We understand this deeply—that all of life is a transformation—and yet, when it comes to our own lives, we fight it.

## The Dark Night of the Soul

Change is frightening because it opens us up to the unknown, which—you guessed it!—is frightening. In spiritual language, this experience is called the **dark night of the soul**: the part of our journey where we enter the unknown and feel surrounded by more questions than answers, more darkness than light.

In the dark night of the soul, we face our own shadows. We face the parts of ourselves that are shrouded in pain, shame, and fear. We are afraid to look at them head-on, convinced that when we do they will terrify us with their snarling teeth and ghoulish eyes. We believe these shadows to be otherworldly, resembling something out of a Hollywood horror movie. We avoid them, look away from them, afraid to meet their gaze.

It was New Year's Eve, and I was sitting in the den of a dark two-bedroom apartment four miles away from my then house. My two-year-old and fifteen-month-old and their father were waiting for me at our neighbors', who were hosting a dinner party. I was running late, but my neighbor, Lea, who is now one of my closest friends, wasn't worried about how long the wait was or why I hadn't shown up with my family. She knew where I was—she sent me there.

As I sat in this small room waiting for what felt like years, my sister sat next to me, both of us full of anticipation. I was sent here and told to ask for Rhea.

"She's a tarot card reader," Lea had told me weeks before. "You have to see her! She's life-changing."

I was curious and terrified. Up until then, I was afraid of all things "supernatural." I didn't want to know things I could never unknow or see something I couldn't unsee. I knew enough about my own intuitive gifts to know that if I dug deeper, I might turn out to be one of those "woo-woos" people made fun of. I sensed things around me, had prophetic dreams, knew when good or bad things were coming—did I really need to also figure out that I could see dead people? No, thank you! People like Rhea scared me, probably because I feared what might be lurking inside myself.

I fidgeted with the couch cushion, bouncing my knee up and down while we waited for Rhea to call us into the room where she'd do my reading.

"Relax," my sister said with an easy smile.

"I am relaxed!" I snapped.

When Rhea finally called us back, she was nothing like how I imagined. Her gentle demeanor, sweet smile, and four-foot-two stature reminded me more of a fairy godmother than the scary witch my Disneyfied brain was expecting.

*She is just a nice lady*, I thought, *no stress.*

We sat down across from her, and she handed me a stack of cards to shuffle. The cards and their frayed edges gave me the distinct impression that Rhea had been at this a long time.

"What's your question?" Rhea asked as I laid down the cards into three neat piles, side by side, like she had instructed.

"Uh, I'm not really sure. I guess I'd just like a general look at my life. If that's something you do," I muttered, a little tentative.

Rhea proceeded to hover her hands over the three piles, seeming to be clearly drawn to one pile, and the reading began. She flipped over the first card and the next, until ten cards were flipped facing up on the table. She took in a deep breath and smiled.

"So, you're divorced?" she asked.

"What? No!" I exclaimed.

"Oh, I'm so sorry, I usually don't see things like that unless they're known to the person I'm doing the reading for. It looked like a positive thing for you," she answered, equally puzzled.

My fight or flight jumped in: *She's going to tell you things you do **not** want to hear, get up and **run***, the fear voice was yelling. I thought of Lea's knowing smile when she told me to come see Rhea. I had been crying to her that day about another fight with my husband, feeling lost and exhausted and hopeless.

I couldn't get up and leave now. This was the answer, and I knew it. I was going to get divorced. Not what I wanted or came to hear. Still, I kept listening.

From that day on, Rhea became a key figure in helping me fully reunite with my Higher Self. She taught me that this reunion is a part of our most difficult life challenges, the point of these darkest nights of the soul we walk through terrified and in deep pain. She also taught me that there's a much more tender part of us trapped in these darker parts.

I'll never forget the first time Rhea led me on a visualization into my own darkness. I was terrified as I sat on her couch with my eyes closed, and we went within to find the pain. I was sure I was not ready to face whatever ghastly creature I found there. This is the monster who had been haunting me, who was driving all my bad decisions, who had led me into a successful but hollow career and a failed, terrible marriage. What could wish so many bad things on me?

My heart thumped loudly in my chest as she directed me to look around the dark, and I started to sense a figure crouched down, hiding from the light somewhere deep in a cave within.

"Shine the light on it," Rhea directed me.

Terrified as I was, I visualized a light shining there where the figure was stooped. I couldn't believe what I saw when the light finally hit her: there, shivering in the shadows, was no demon or monster. It was me, age six, terrified and alone. I felt overwhelmed by tenderness for this little girl. I wanted so badly to wrap my arms around her and protect her from the loneliness of that cave. It was a feeling of love I can only compare to how I feel about my kids when they are sad or need me. Loving ourselves like this has become my new definition of healing.

You see, these shadows within that we try so hard to avoid feel familiar because they *are* familiar. These aspects that we see as our darkness are just our younger selves trapped in their pain and in their shame. If only we were taught that all along. Then we would know what to do with them. Instead of confusing these shadows with our current reality, we would see them for what they are: a projection of past suffering waiting to be healed. In confusing these past beliefs and pains with our current reality, we believe wholeheartedly that what's being projected in the dark, all those painful moments, are on the verge of coming to life and engulfing us fully.

In my own life and in coaching many others through their own dark night of the soul, I know that when we don't understand this experience as the *healing* part of our spiritual journey, we lose ourselves in it. We act out. We don't seek our truth. We only exist to make the pain go away. This is often where so many of my clients fall into paranoia about the actions of their co-founders, producers, directors, partners, coworkers and so on. Instead of reaching into the darkness to find the most tender and frightened parts of themselves, they act out from the fears that exist in that darkness.

Their limiting beliefs convince them that they aren't valued and, therefore, not safe in community with their colleagues; instead of seeing those beliefs as projections from a much younger and fearful part within, they believe the projections to be their current reality and become defensive. This is the source of all conflict, in my experience. Our tiniest, most frightened selves become triggered and instead of taking the time to take care of them, we react and lash out as an act of protection.

How many decisions do we make driven by the fear of that little kid cowering in the cave? That kid can't see clearly, buried beneath all the pain or confusion they've experienced. All they know is that they aren't safe, so they project this paranoia into our present. Without finding and integrating that part of us back into a healed space within our present selves, that scared, paranoid little voice will always try to convince us not to trust others and we act out from that place.

I spend a lot of time walking people back into the cave to reclaim this lost, little part of themselves. This is a deeply transformative moment in our work—when I get to see my clients embrace this self and learn that instead of listening to its scared projections, all they need to do is see and love this aspect. I genuinely see their relationships with others change after this moment. Once they identify the scared self and the way it projects limiting beliefs about their relationship to others, they also learn to tune into their intuitive knowing and take action with others from this place of healed wisdom instead of fear.

Interacting with others out of fear is what breeds toxicity in our behavior. It is what allows us to treat others so horribly. When we believe the projections of this scared self, we act like the dangerous creature in the cave I was so afraid I'd find on my own journey into the shadow self. Remember when I told you earlier that one of my main rules when interacting with other people's toxicity is to remember it's never about you? This is why. When you see people behave in a harmful way, this is the source. This unhealed, terrified, shameful little self, shivering in some dark corner within.

The other alternative to this paranoid toxicity I see people project is a complete and total disregard of their boundaries. Believing their limiting beliefs about themselves, they're motivated to prove they're valuable by doing what they believe others want instead of what they need. They say no when they mean yes, or yes when they mean no. This is how we lose our way and land in places we never meant to be.

One of my favorite lessons lies in this space. It's called the **full body yes.** To help my clients change this behavior of doing the opposite of what they want or need as a way to receive love, I tell them they have to follow one rule during our work together, as my husband once said to me: "If it's not a *fuck yes*, then it's a *no*." That simple.

If you're asked to do something and you aren't screaming *YES!* from the inside, then the answer is no. No matter how uncomfortable it feels, I ask my clients to say no and to keep saying no until it's easier and easier to do. It does get easier, by the way. Anything we practice with repetition gets easier. Saying no is no different.

Stop for a second and check in with yourself. Do either of these strategies, of paranoia toward others or nonexistent boundaries, sound familiar in your own life? What shadows within are so scary that instead of face them head-on, you project them outward by using one of these two strategies?

In the midst of a professional crisis, one of my clients found out that her husband was filing for divorce. After months of work on finding her **full body yes,** only saying yes when she meant it and not out of a place of need or desperation, being faced with losing her job and her partner at the same time suddenly sent her right back to her old coping strategy of accepting anything that made her feel safe and valuable instead of checking in with her truest needs and worth.

She started considering opportunities that bored her, roles that were way too small or limited for who she is and what she'd accomplished in her career. The pain from life crashing down on her signaled to her limiting beliefs that they needed to take over. We had promised those parts of her that they could take a break. They no longer needed to protect her from pain and then, bam! Gut-wrenching pain.

It is *so* hard to have faith in the work in these moments. It's so hard for our younger selves, poised to jump into action to protect us from pain, to not do what they've been trained to do. It's so easy to forget that we can't let them into the driver's seat, that there is meaning behind the heartbreak—in whatever form it arrives.

"Why is this all happening at once?" she'd ask in our sessions. It felt so unfair that there existed a universe where she'd have to go through two dramatic heartbreaks simultaneously.

"You're in your dark night of the soul," I told her. "Your pain is real, so feel it, but also know that what is being taken is falling away because you have outgrown it and are ready for the next chapter, where your soul can come even more into its desires."

I knew that this wouldn't take her hurt away in the moment; when we are in the dark night, we can convince ourselves that daylight is lost to us, that life is just unfair. While in the dark night, we really forget that things are working out in our favor behind the scenes, because they feel like the exact opposite. That's when it's helpful to remind ourselves that what is no longer meant for us has to fade to make room for all that is coming.

I sometimes look back on the era of my divorce, where everything was falling apart, where I entered my own dark night of the soul, and marvel at just how much darkness I was surrounded by. As if the disintegration of my marriage wasn't enough, my job at that time was literally managing crisis. In some ways, maybe the crises of these clients made my own life seem less hectic and painful. Maybe it allowed me an escape. Even so, it was a *lot* to manage.

Whatever it was, I would spend days, weeks even, talking to angry, frightened, devastated leaders. For each of them, things had been moving along wonderfully, they'd tell me, and then, out of nowhere, everything began to fall apart. It was always the same story: "Everything was fine, until it wasn't."

I learned two things through my work at that time. First, there were always warning signs, always whispers from their Higher Self, and from others. They'd say things like "I just had a gut feeling but I wasn't sure where it came" or "People started pointing out issues in our system but we were up against a tight deadline so we had to keep moving forward."

Second, most of these situations were made worse because the dark night of the soul had them in a terror grip. Projections of devastating worse-case scenarios from their most frightened selves made them choose to stay silent when they should have spoken up, or inactive when they should have taken action. By the time they thought to call in the experts, many of them had already succumbed to the pull of their reinvigorated limiting belief systems about themselves. The fear and shame bubbled up around them, surrounding them, drowning them in a sea of self-doubt.

From this place, they made, most often, some pretty bad decisions. They took their dark night of the soul experience, this projection of past pain and shame, and externalized it. Instead of seeing the inner shadows as spaces that needed their loving attention, they fed them by reacting from their guidance. Defensiveness, shutting down, lashing out—all behaviors guided by a part of them that just wanted to be healed but was instead put into the driver's seat.

This happened a lot at the firm where I worked: reactivity from a place of deep inner shame. It was probably thanks to the pressure to perform, without honoring our own truth above all else, we all found ourselves under. We had to ignore our inner wisdom so much that sometimes we forgot ourselves. In place of our humanity, we'd fill our heads with ideas about the kind of personality it took to be respected or powerful in a high-powered environment like that. Full of these ideas we walked around like we owned the world . . . and then, just like my clients I was advising, bam! Out of nowhere someone would have a personal crisis. Enter dark night of the soul.

Except, no one had time to heal what was asking to be healed. I've never seen so much lashing out in my life. Everyone was desperate to ignore the limiting beliefs and the shame that came to a head during a moment of crisis, projecting it all outward toward anyone but themselves. We hurt each other. We said terrible things to each other because we believed them about ourselves.

In those years I was called "aggressive" or "scary." Sometimes, when I'd be promoted and someone else wouldn't, I'd get the *look at her, caring about her career more than her kids* treatment. Projections. Sometimes just by existing, I offended people. I will never forget the time a female executive who outranked me called me a "breeder" to my face because I had to leave a happy hour early to get to my kids. Now I look back on her and wonder what dark night of the soul she was in. What was asking to be healed that instead came out as a hurtful jab about two little people in my life I so adored?

The bottom line is: You can't ignore the dark night of the soul. There is no amount of projecting it outward that will make it go away. There is only going inward. We must learn to love our dark nights, to love the shadowy parts of us lurking beneath because they've been told they are ugly. They are asking for our gaze, for our attention, and ultimately for the loving guidance of our Higher Selves. They know we have that aspect to us. They've experienced Higher Self too, and what they want more than anything is its powerful, loving embrace.

That desire to be healed, coupled with our Higher Self's desire for our own expansion, is often what creates these crises, these phoenix moments. Without them, we would keep sleepwalking through the cardboard lives we created out of our need to conform. If these experiences didn't show up with such drama, they wouldn't get our attention. We are too comfortable in what we've constructed to give it up to heal and expand.

Every crisis is an opportunity to pick up the pieces and realign our lives in the image of our truth instead of a false reality we've been conditioned toward. If we don't live in our truth, the ultimate goal of our Higher Self, the crisis will show up to blow it all to bits so we have no choice but to do exactly that.

The healing and the expansion must occur so we can evolve, so what other choice does our soul have but to force us to do so? But we naturally take these painful moments personally. We shout at the universe, "What the hell did I do to deserve this!" If the universe could answer back in a language we understood, it would say, *You asked for this. Somewhere deep inside, you wanted more. I'm giving you a pathway to more.*

This is your wake-up call. Whatever phoenix process or dark night of the soul you're in, it's not meant to hurt you. Rather, it's an invitation. It's calling to you, saying, *Remember me? Take my hand, let's find out who you are. Let's get you what you truly want.*

It's your time to listen.

### Freeing the Monster from the Cave

My dark night of the soul led me out of the cave into the arms of a life that I had no evidence was even possible. I would have never gone in and healed the little lonely girl who didn't believe she was worthy of love had the world not come crashing down on my head in my early thirties. It was the sheer pain of it all that pushed me to do whatever it took to just start to feel better, and that led to my inner journey.

That healing moved me from heartbreak to the most supportive marriage I have ever seen. It pushed me out of a job where my skills were being used for other people's gain instead of my own well-being. Had the dark night of the soul not arrived for me, I don't know where I'd be. Still in a marriage where I couldn't really be my Higher Self? Stuck in a job where I was never truly seen and still believing that success meant sacrificing my own truth to make others proud of me? Of course, I couldn't see it then, when I'd lay on the floor of my bedroom crying into a pillow so I didn't wake the kids.

But it helped me to have Rhea reminding me that there was a purpose to it all. Actually, she told me that I was walking that dark path so I could one day help others who were in their dark night. I can't say I believed her then, but I can't really deny it now, can I?

EXPLORATION: *Your Deepest Fear*

This is your moment to face whatever is lurking in your shadows head-on, knowing that just by looking at it, it will become less daunting. Use the following prompts to courageously face what you currently fear:

1. What is something that you fear most right now? Is there a decision you've been putting off in your career, relationship, family, or friendships? What are the parts of your life that you can sense a change needs to happen? Write about it.

2. How are your younger selves, the limiting beliefs, influencing you to feel about what's causing you pain? What do they want you to do about it?

3. Bringing in that clear, knowing feeling, ask yourself this: *What could be the purpose of this pain? What might be on the other side? What comes to you?* Write about it.

CHAPTER 8

# Confusing a Job with Our Purpose

*Higher Self is waiting as* we continue on our little path—you know, the one laid out for us by others. Before it can really make its entrance, there's one more life event it must try to patiently, albeit invisibly, guide us through: our careers.

I should know. I made it especially hard for my Higher Self to reach me, something I hope to help other people avoid. I had left my marriage and had clear evidence for choosing Higher Self, and still when it came to the way I made money, I had to go through the entire dance of learning to trust her over my fear, again. Rhea had told me my purpose was to heal, but I couldn't see the pathway, so I made the mistake I think so many do, settling for an external definition of success over my internal truth.

I worked at a "desk" job in corporate America for close to twenty years—*desk* being in quotes because, for most of that time, I was on the road visiting clients. In those twenty years, I worked at PR and marketing agencies. I was a brand manager, a reputation strategist, a crisis manager, a PR executive, a marketing executive . . . a lot of things that pretty much amounted to the same thing: helping leaders make people trust them and their companies.

For a long time, I loved this work. I found the challenges exciting, and I liked figuring out how to tell stories in a way that persuaded people to see things "our way." But I absolutely hated the way corporate culture made me feel, and the things I had to sacrifice about myself to succeed. There are so many "norms" in work culture we accept that are harmful to our sense of self-worth. Every time I came up against one, I bristled. Common, day-to-day work occurrences felt like exercises in stroking other people's egos and a downright waste of time to me.

Working past 5 p.m. to show how dedicated I was one of these things. I never saw the point of missing out on my life so I could prove to someone else I mattered. So, I left at 5 p.m. or even 4 p.m. a lot to go spend time with my young kids. Sometimes that meant I'd have to speak up and ask supervisors for more realistic deadlines, other times it meant not reacting to the temptation to volunteer to do extra work to show my worth, and other times it meant learning to delegate as a leader and give others the opportunity to work with me instead of controlling the work product so tightly.

Besides, I knew I added value. Somehow, work was the one place I didn't often look for other people's validation, and I often refused to play into the culture. Maybe that was because I was a woman, a brown woman, climbing my way up a corporate ladder through a sea of white men. I think I learned that if I stopped to consider what other people thought of me, or how my unconventional existence disheartened them, I'd get stuck, or held back, and I wasn't going to let that happen.

I'll never forget the time a leader in my organization called my boss to tell him I was "overly aggressive" because I had advocated for my team in a situation that was blatantly unfair to them.

"Would he have said that about you in the same situation?" I asked my boss when he brought the "feedback" to me.

That shut him up real fast.

This happened a lot. Once, the head of our office came upstairs, where I sat with my hundred-person team, to tell me people downstairs on the other teams were "scared" of me. Scared? Why? Because I said what I thought? Because I didn't let people mistreat my employees?

I look back on it now and don't quite know how I didn't let that shake me as a young woman in a male-dominated field. It almost buoyed me to hear it. I remember thinking to myself, *If they need to be scared of me to treat my people well, then so be it.*

So, there was the misogyny and the racism that I had to fend off, and I did, but even still, there were things I had to endure that drained my soul. Things that weren't my job itself but made me feel consistently less comfortable within that work culture. Things like sitting through long meetings just to help a supervisor process their own thoughts out loud, or prove they had power, while a mountain of work piled up for me on my desk. Or, taking the blame for someone else's mistake because of their position in a hierarchy over me. Or, making clients, or worse, higher-ups in my own agency feel like they were brilliant, even when they had terrible ideas. Just nonsense that became a part of operating in corporate culture that I couldn't escape. Not if I wanted to move up. This stuff ate away at me over time, and it finally reached a boiling point thanks to my Higher Self breaking through clearly to put her foot down: we'd had enough.

It was 2017 and I was years out of my divorce, was busting my ass as a single mother who was solely responsible for the financial care of both kids. It had paid off. I was the global head of strategy at the world's largest private PR firm. It was my dream job. A job I fought hard to get. But lately, the job didn't *feel* like a dream anymore. More days than not, the pressure to agree with the collective instead of listening to my inner wisdom became gut-wrenching.

The days of excitement for the three-hour Acela ride from Washington, DC, to New York and subsequent Uber drive along the West Side Highway began to feel like a distant memory. In those days, the butterflies in my stomach would flutter with anticipation at the opportunity that lay ahead in that gorgeous building.

The idea that I, an Iranian American woman who was most unlike the rest of my colleagues, had the ear and attention of one of the world's most prominent agency CEOs buoyed my every step.

*This* was what I always wanted. To be seen. With this job, I had access to the world's biggest brands, extravagant business trips around the world, and clout. The kind that made people notice when I showed up, knowing that something important must be happening in that building on Hudson Street just from the sound of my gold bangles jingling down the hallways. Everything I wanted and yet . . . those butterflies seemed to have fallen asleep and been replaced with an unending void. The kind that calls and calls with such aching persistence that it dulls the previously colorful things around you into gray.

On this particular day, I enter the conference room across from the CEO's desk with a sense of dread mixed with a longing to escape. Immediately I feel everyone's nerves as they sit in the room waiting for him to arrive and start the meeting. At our office, "What's the weather today?" was code for asking about his mood.

*Why do we care so much?* I found an unruly voice asking from deep inside me. *Don't we know what needs to be done regardless of how he's feeling? Do we always need to be reacting? Don't we have our own internal compass anymore?* I started to notice that these shifting moods from our leader became our only compass. Instead of clearheaded thinking or creativity, things you can only access when you're in alignment with your inner wisdom, we'd scramble to please him, which made us hugely reactive and not as innovative or as wise as I believed we were.

What was happening? Where were these rebellious thoughts coming from? *Shake it off and focus,*" I told myself. But it just wasn't that easy. The work we were doing was losing its allure. I know now that this was by design. I wasn't fully living in my purpose or embracing my gifts, so I had to become disillusioned to move away from my work, but at the time I felt it had more to do with the environment I was in.

I started to notice that the higher up I moved in the firm, all of us were just planets that revolved around the sun, our CEO. That when our ideas and skills served his vision, we were embraced, but that as soon as they didn't, we were disposable. I watched what a system like that does to people who define their value by the amount of power they can accumulate in that environment. The executive committee put in place to help steer us and our clients toward good work became instead a bad reenactment of *The Hunger Games*. Who could get the CEO to listen to them most that quarter?

The answer to that question defined not only the fate of the lucky winner(s), but the rest of us too. If you were on the right side of that game, your career advanced and your relationships thrived. If not, your life became a fight for survival, and you were the prey. This did not bring out the best in most people. In fighting for relevance, they would become controlling and defensive.

Instead of seeing each other as valuable cocreators, we saw each other as competition. We believed in scarcity. We believed that there was so little recognition and value to go around that we had to scratch and claw at each other to get a drop of that precious resource. Which took empathy right out of the equation. We didn't really see each other anymore. People were either assets or obstacles.

I couldn't live that way. I couldn't live with the changing winds, *YOU ARE AMAZING* switching to *YOU ARE NOT ENOUGH* at the blink of an eye. A rebellion was forming in me because I was, I realize now, tired of the game.

That particular day, as these dangerous thoughts ran through my mind, we talked, like we always did, about the amazing work the firm was doing around the idea of trust. Each year, our firm put out a report that made us the industry-leading source on what consumers around the world trusted—or didn't—about business and other institutions. The methodology was painstaking and produced highly valuable data for marketers who looked to earn loyalty from their customers. Every year, we'd roll out the results of this survey to fanfare from the media and our clients.

*Trust in business is everything*, we'd say.

But here's the issue: We didn't trust ourselves. We didn't trust ourselves enough to say no when a client wanted something that wasn't right for them. We didn't trust ourselves enough to say no when our CEO's mood swings demanded that we make promises to those same clients that we couldn't keep. How could we teach other leaders to elicit trust when we didn't intrinsically understand trust as a concept? We were saying the right things and making them look pretty.

That was the moment it hit me. Sitting in that conference room, feeling the exhaustion of the twelve years I spent at this agency working sixty-hour weeks to get myself at this table, I thought: **We are doing it all wrong**.

We would never actually connect these leaders to the people that mattered in a way that mattered. Trust from customers, employees, shareholders, whoever, starts with trust in yourself as a leader, as a person. We would always be one step short because we weren't starting by establishing this most important connection to self. And we couldn't do *that* because we had each traded our connection to ourselves—our Higher Self—for the opportunity to sit around this elusive table. We were separated from our all-knowing selves and operating at a lesser capacity to make others feel more comfortable.

*Well, shit*, I thought, *how can companies be trusted to do the right thing, ever, when all the decision-makers are so disconnected from their inner wisdom?*

This, I realized in that moment, was what the inner voice was trying to tell me. What felt like a void inside wasn't one after all; it was a familiar voice calling to me, saying: *You know better. Do better.*

### Assimilation into Corporate Culture

I, just like you, had a deep connection to my Higher Self when I was younger. I was always aware of it. From the moment I could first remember, I seemed to have a knowing about things. I could walk into a room and feel people's pain, fear, joy, anxiety, or any emotion they were having so deeply that for years I couldn't tell the difference between other people's thoughts and feelings and my own. I learned much later that this power had a name, *empath*, and that being an empath was part of my Higher Self.

But there were other parts too. Parts of me that knew things would happen before they did or knew a solution to a complicated problem almost instantly. Over time, I learned to name this ability as my **intuition**. I knew what it felt like. I always heard it, but I often ignored it when it came to my own life. When it came to my *work*, though, I used intuition all the time with every client who needed a solution, was facing a crisis, or wanted desperately to connect to their customers. I knew I used intuition, but never would I dare utter this out loud. I was a serious business strategist, not some loon who talked to unseen voices.

That day as I sat in the New York office, Higher Self getting louder and louder, running the past twelve years through my head like a movie, I realized something profound: *This connection I had to my Higher Self was what I'd used to guide these powerful Fortune 500 leaders and my own teams all along.* My intuition wasn't a woo-woo character flaw; this was my gift.

I could always sense who people really were deep inside and what they really wanted to say or do. What I had been doing all this time, without really knowing it, was guiding them closer to their own wisdom, their own Higher Self. When I was called in to solve a problem, I felt that I knew the answer from somewhere deep within me. However, my method had always been to lead by asking the right questions, unearthing slowly the glimmer within each of them that knew what to do all along. Once this connection was established, they became unstoppable.

Unfortunately, that glimmer had been so buried by the *can't*s and *shouldn't*s of corporate America that many of these leaders had lost their way. So profoundly, in fact, that mistakes were made, big and small, and customers and employees ended up hurt. Through the years, these executives began to believe that the only way to success was to pay big bucks and surround themselves with gads of highly paid experts to tell them what to do—all instead of finding the answers from within.

Looking at my clients and my own firm in this new way made it hard not to see that I had lost my way too. I had become a corporate zombie, someone who followed spoken and unspoken rules to prove her value. I knew what I had to do and say and exactly who I needed to be to chase that next promotion, and that person was not my unadulterated self. I was playing a part.

I knew that to get the raise, acquire a higher rank, or accumulate more power within the organization, there was no way I could live awake to my own deepest truths or to my purpose. The two could not live side by side. The world I was living in, the one that was paying my salary, had no room for the full self. That world required a half-self, one that blended my natural skills and talents with a blueprint for success that asked me to turn off so much of my individuality, which included that deep empathy and intuitive wisdom.

In those days and in that firm, conformity meant security. If you showed too much empathy, it was perceived as weakness. Someone would swoop in from another office or team and pull your account out from under you. If you felt in your bones that something was right or wrong, but your client or the CEO disagreed, you told that knowing part of you to shut up and you did what you were being told to do. There was no room for inner wisdom or deep, heart-centered compassion toward yourself or toward others. Conforming to the norms led to the desired results; doing otherwise wasn't an option.

*You know better, do better.* My Higher Self grew louder every day as these realizations came pouring in. Once I really listened and made the decision inside myself to leave my job, her guidance went from vague to detailed. I realized seemingly out of the blue one day that all I needed to do was start to ask myself, *If you were running the show, what kind of work would you be doing?*

That was a question from my Higher Self; I know that now

because the answer to that question has led me to the practice I've now built. I knew, with all the responsibility on my shoulders, that I couldn't just leap off a cliff, so I started engaging in the conversation with Higher Self slowly, just like I had with the end of my marriage.

I registered an LLC—Eight22 Group—named after my birthday. I went on Squarespace and built a little website and used that website to work out exactly what I wanted to say, who I wanted to help, and how I wanted to apply my skills. I started talking about what I was building to anyone who would listen.

All the while, I still worked hard at my agency job, but every evening, I spent an hour on my dream. I dared let myself dream from a place of my truest wants and needs and I waited.

Then the day came; an organization I was introduced to through a friend needed some help managing some internal chaos, and without realizing these words were about to come out of my mouth I asked, "What if instead of working through my agency, you worked directly with me?"

That was my first client in my new coaching endeavor and two weeks later I told my agency it was time to part ways.

## Imposter Syndrome

If you work in a corporate job, I'm willing to bet you're somewhere on this spectrum of parting with your own truth. That's what the corporate world is designed for: maximum efficiency. You maximize profit and minimize cost. This naturally creates a domino effect. To make the maximum profit, they hire fewer people than what's needed to get the job done. But you as their employee can't know that, so they have to convince you that this lack of resourcing is by design. They convince you of this by touting a hard work ethic as a shiny gold star that will set you apart and make you more valuable. So, you work sixty to eighty hours a week to prove you're worth it.

Corporations validate this by creating promotion processes and salary bands that show us "evidence" that working even harder is the only way we can be better compensated, so we keep pushing. Companies aren't going to say, *Hey, profit is what we're after here, so we're going to ask you to do the job of two or three people to save us costs.* Instead, they say, *Don't you want it bad enough? Aren't you motivated? Look at so-and-so over here, she's working on weekends!*

So, you push and contort yourself to fit whatever box they've constructed and named their corporate "culture." You work hard and keep measuring yourself against an unreachable standard that has little to do with your truth, wisdom, or purpose. Once again, another system in your life that's telling you that you aren't enough as you are.

This cycle is even worse as an immigrant; I've watched it firsthand with my parents. People don't leave their homes if everything they need and want already exists there; my parents—and many other immigrants—made those big, life-changing moves in the hopes of a better life. This is something I wish everyone could truly understand. Why leave the comfort of your own home, language, culture and the understanding of who you are culturally, unless there is something lacking where you are? You wouldn't.

Immigrants come to their new home with the goal of making life better for themselves and their families. If, in this drive toward better, they are met with scarcity of resources and security, this motivation can turn easily to desperation. Who's there to play on this desperation? That's right—the exact same system that tells all of us that hard work proves our value.

Sadly, in this case, the power dynamics are even more overt, from indoctrination to exploitation. This isn't just true for immigrants, unfortunately. It is the experience of most minorities anywhere; whether that status be based on race, gender, class, or any facet of our identity, the working world has long used the tactic of exploiting a deep hunger for security and dignity as a prod to push people beyond their limits to maximize profit.

I see this a lot with my clients who identify as female. Whether they are CEOs, agents, authors, or performers, these clients are the ones who are most likely to put in the extra time, pick up other people's responsibilities, and solve problems way beyond their pay grade most consistently. This is a complicated onion, layered with root causes and limiting beliefs. However, I truly believe that this is the experience of my female-identifying leaders because, in addition to all the limiting beliefs they've been taught about themselves, the working world also tells them they have to do more to get the same results as their male counterparts.

This external messaging to female-identified people is the clearest form of exploiting a drive for success that I see daily. Knowing that those who identify as female want it badly, knowing they've been held back for far too long historically, our working world has no problem asking them to do more, because we know they will say yes. If that's not exploiting someone's hunger for being valued, I don't know what is.

Regardless of whether you have the immigrant experience, or your parents have, or you're nowhere near connected to that experience, the results are the same; this system of profit over people convinces you that you're not enough, again. You're so used to not being enough by this point in your life, you accept it easily. Even if you don't think it overtly, there's a part of your subconscious that's so familiar with that story, it feels comfortable to accept it as truth.

Every time you have a great idea that's struck down thoughtlessly by a visionless (or insecure) manager, You *are not enough* raises its head.

When you watch a colleague who doesn't carry their weight get promoted over you, *You are not enough* shows up.

When you work up the courage to ask for a raise and get the runaround about how you need to improve your performance, *You are not enough* expands itself within.

And, since you're in an environment that doesn't fully encourage free thinking, intuitive wisdom, or deep empathy, that limiting belief system has a chance to truly flourish. It is that story, that good old limiting belief system about yourself that's been quietly operating within you from childhood, that allows you to accept these ridiculous circumstances. In the working world, that story, *I am not enough*, sprouts into a full-blown crisis, reflected on every single one of my clients' faces as **imposter syndrome**.

Imposter syndrome shows up differently for each of us. What comes up for you when you hear those two words? What does it mean specifically in your life? For most of my clients and myself, imposter syndrome is the belief that the thing we've been given the chance to do, we are not inherently worthy of or prepared for. We believe that there is someone far better suited to it than us. That in doing that thing, we are somehow pretending to be good at it.

My training to believe this voice comes from my time in corporate America. In the working world, you are striving for some version of yourself that always remains just out of reach. Do you know why it remains so elusive? Because that image you are striving to reach was never created for you. That image of obedient perfection was created to motivate you to do what needs to be done so the business can succeed. Of course you feel like an imposter when you continue to chase a mirage.

Here's the truth: There is no such thing as perfection. Perfection is a myth. If you look up the definition of *perfection* you'll find this: "the condition, state, or quality of being free or as free as possible from all flaws or defects."

Well, who decides what's a flaw and a defect? Isn't it convenient for another system that needs you to work for its own success to define those flaws and defects? If your qualities don't produce the optimal outcome for the business, is that an inherent flaw in you? Not only is your value being defined by the outside, in all the ways we've talked about so far, but so are your flaws. Of course we feel like imposters when we're trying to achieve the impossible image of perfection.

We are human, and we are here to grow. The areas we need to grow into are illuminated through the opportunities we receive to interact with others and with ourselves. Are these flaws? I don't see them that way, and I want you to stop letting other people tell

## Confusing a Job with Our Purpose

you that's what they are. I want you to wake up to the truth that you are a work in progress.

You are here to reunite with your Higher Self, the limitless, wise, and purposeful aspect of you. The only way to do that is to learn, and the only way to learn is through trial and error. The fact that we have people watching that human experience of trial and error and convincing us there's something flawed in us because our process isn't happening fast enough for them is cruel, it is limiting, and it needs to become unacceptable for you.

Here's the punch line: those that try to convince you that you're flawed because you're imperfect can only do that because there is a deep, internal judgment about themselves. Believe me, there is not one single person who does not feel that they are somehow an imposter. This is why imposter syndrome is a joke; we're all walking around thinking someone else has it figured it out while that someone is looking at yet another someone thinking the same, and on and on.

The other truth I learned after more than a decade trying hard to win in environments that asked me to shrink is that this form of control only benefits one set of people: the ones with their names on the door. We're taught that treating each other with judgment and lack of empathy at work is normal. That seeing each other as competition is healthy. We're taught that there's only one right way to do things and we watch people who master that way of behaving, without checking in with their own integrity, be rewarded.

All of this is painstakingly ingrained in us so that we can leave our truth in the corner and morph into perfect clones of each other, working toward one thing: maximum profit with minimum investment. That's what success is defined as in boardrooms and investor meetings. How much profit can be made with as little investment as possible in the people helping make that profit? And it's a brilliant strategy! You know why? Because the *I'm not enough* within each of us is always looking for proof that this core wound is true. What's the most foolproof way to get people to work hard for you without questioning whether there's an equitable transfer of money or power? To play on their darkest, most shame-filled thoughts about themselves.

"Yes," they say, "you are not enough. But you know how you might start to become enough? Right this way."

So, what do you do with all this information if you're in the working world today? I know you can't just walk in tomorrow and demand that everyone see and respect your truth. But you know what you can do?

You can awaken to the truth yourself.

You can awaken to that truth while clearly seeing once and for all that the standards you're being asked to meet have nothing to do with getting you closer to your purpose.

You can make a decision from this newly informed, wide-awake place that it's your job, and your job only, to understand, embody, and live your purpose no matter what.

You can decide today that your life is about understanding and living your purpose so that your needs, desires, and passions can coexist with your desire for success.

Because they can. And it all starts with understanding your purpose clearly.

## Refusing to Lose Yourself

You don't have to accept the norms of the working world to thrive within it. You are reading this book because, as Gandhi once said, you are ready to "be the change you wish to see in the world." I won't lie and tell you this part is easy, but someday when you've had enough, it will become easier than shrinking to fit the tight mold set before you by those who shape your career.

As part of my coaching, I help leaders figure out how to do this and how to encourage their teams to live and work in this way. I'm what's called a "coach in residence" for several organizations, or, as most of these clients call me, the "work therapist." In these arrangements, every leader within the organization has agreed to work with me, both individually and as a group. It only really works when I'm coaching the entire leadership team, so that each person with high-level power and responsibility at the company becomes accountable to changing together.

The first part of this work is focused on unlearning old, toxic dynamics they've learned from our current corporate culture. We start by coaching one-on-one so I can work with each leader to uncover which specific limiting beliefs are activated within each of them and make a clear link about how those beliefs are causing them to enact harm to themselves and their coworkers.

This step is important. Without this self-awareness, there can be no change. Toxicity in a workplace, or any space, for that matter, always begins with the one(s) who holds the most power. Once those people see the pathway from their own pain to their current patterns of harming others, they can't unsee it. They, usually, begin to change their habits, big and small, which creates a massive reverb across the organization.

But most of the time, these leaders don't just come to the conclusion that they will suddenly undergo this hard work of self-discovery and change on their own. Usually, it comes once their employees show that they won't accept anything less. Sometimes employees leave in large numbers, or put up strong boundaries collectively, or generally just complain enough that the leaders realize it's do-or-die time. Whichever path brings them to me, usually by the time these leaders show up, they are worried about losing the people that help make their companies a success, because those people have spoken up, loud and clear.

I'm telling you this because I want you to understand just how empowered you are, no matter which part of the power structure you fit into. As a leader, you are empowered to heal your shadow self so that your organization can thrive without terrifying skeletons threatening to burst out of the closet. As an employee, you're empowered to create change by choosing not to believe the evidence for *I'm not enough* that you find when you go looking for it, and instead asking yourself, *What do I need to really feel like I'm valued here? Where do I need to say yes or no to make sure my needs are met?* And finally, *How is this job allowing me to express my purpose?*

I will go into more detail on the specific actions you can take to align to your Higher Self at work later. However, before I leave you here in the career phase of your life, I want to provide you with the first three rules of aligning to your Higher Self at work that I share with my clients:

1. **BLIND AGREEMENT IS NOT PRODUCTIVE.** Always make sure you take a moment to locate within yourself how an idea, thought, or action you're being asked to take stacks up against your own beliefs, values, and needs. You may be asked to do something that absolutely goes against your values, in a room full of people who are nodding along, collectively agreeing it's the right thing to do. If in that moment you feel heaviness in your chest or the pit of your stomach that comes with knowing something is wrong but not speaking up, feel that pressure and recognize it as a sign that you have to voice your dissent. Disagreement is not destructive. When you take the time to get honest with yourself about what you really think, speaking up from that place of clarity is incredibly powerful. Often, you'll find that your leaders, colleagues, or investors will take a minute to consider your point of view and might even find this different way of looking at the same problem refreshing or even more effective.

2. **MARTYRS BELONG IN DOCTRINE, NOT IN THE WORKPLACE.** You can sacrifice yourself as much as you want; it will never make them truly see you. Instead, people get used to you playing the role of martyr and start to expect you to put your needs aside to take care of theirs. This is true in all parts of your life, by the way—and especially at work. Your temptation to martyr yourself is coming from the limiting belief that says your needs don't matter, that if you put other people's needs and expectations before your own, you will be loved and valued. It's an illusion, and it never works out that way. What are you giving up to be the one everyone can count on? Just start, for now, to make a list of those sacrifices and then ask yourself these questions for each sacrifice you make: 1. What's the cost of this to me? 2. What's the benefit? Do the benefits outweigh the costs? Just become

aware; that's all you need to do. Remember, once you see it, you can't unsee it. The change will come organically from this simple state of awareness.

3. **IT IS NEVER ABOUT YOU, EVER.** People want you to believe that it is. It's easier that way. That way, they don't have to deal with the real pain inside of themselves. They can project that pain onto you. You don't have to let them. Know this: that boss or coworker who makes you feel irrelevant, worthless, or stupid—those are feelings and beliefs they hold toward themselves. This is true 100 percent of the time. Trust me. We are too self-centered a species to think of something unless it is within us, which means unless we feel or think something about ourselves, there is absolutely no way we can feel or think it about someone else. Next time you're in a situation where someone at work speaks to you disrespectfully, before you believe their projections, just stop for a moment and ask yourself, How would I behave if I was sure they were actually saying these things about themselves? You might have some empathy and compassion for them from this new perspective, but that's not what I'm asking you to do yet. Right now, I just want you to use this new perspective to distance yourself from the harsh words and attitudes. You'll get to compassion eventually, but for now, I want you to put a barrier up around yourself. Don't let other people offload the burden of their inner darkness onto you. Notice it, put it in its appropriate category of "their shit," and shake it right off your shoulders. More on how to do this later, I promise.

## The Purpose Equation

When people tell me they've been laid off or fired, I get excited for them. Okay, hold on: I know it's terrifying. I know our sense of well-being and security comes under attack when our livelihood is taken away by someone else. I am not taking that lightly. I remember my mom getting laid off when she was our sole provider. We didn't go to the grocery store for weeks. Losing your job is not a joke. It can be life or death.

Yet, there's a destination awaiting us at the end of this path that can be life-changing. If we use this moment of crisis as an opportunity, the destination is always, 100 percent of the time better than where we started.

Here's why: When we hold ourselves up from achieving our dreams and living our purpose out of fear and limiting beliefs, the universe gets a little impatient watching us waste our shimmer on circumstances that are beneath our frequency. It will, from time to time, when we fail to take the leap, lovingly yet abruptly push us off the cliff we've been peering over tentatively to catapult us toward our destiny. (I say the same thing about divorces and breakups too, by the way, but we'll save that for later.) After doing this sort of work with the universe for years, I am here to tell you this: when one part of your career ends abruptly, it's a sign that you were no longer on your purpose path and it's time to get back on track.

Here's the most important thing to know about purpose: the idea that your purpose is a hobby or requires you to give up aspirations for success in favor of living like a monk is a myth that's been created by people who want you to work for their dreams rather than for your own.

Think on that for a moment.

If you were told, from the moment you began to think about a career, that your career *had to be linked to your purpose*, would you have made different decisions? We're often told that to be successful, we need to be practical, to follow a predetermined path that assures us success. People in power love that because they get your magic all for themselves. You are taught to channel your magic into their dreams because you are made to believe that this is the most practical path to your own success. This is 100 percent untrue.

I am beyond proud and grateful for the insanely talented and noteworthy people I get to guide every day. I can also tell you that each and every one of them only became successful or noteworthy after they began truly doing what they loved and were meant to do.

Let me guess your next question: How am I supposed to know what I'm meant to do when I've been taught all this time not to think about it? I love this question! This is where the exploration begins.

It starts with a simple equation:

*The Purpose Equation: Natural Skills + the Experience of Joy or Fulfillment = Positive Impact on Others*

Your purpose is the reason you exist, in this specific moment in this specific body with the exact traits and desires you have. When you do the things you are naturally good at, you derive a natural sense of fulfillment from those things and in doing that, you have an impact on the world around you. How you express your purpose can change dozens of times throughout your life and even in any given day.

Let's say you're naturally a nurturing person who finds caring for others really fulfilling. You can express that nurturing in hundreds of ways. You could be in your purpose walking down the street and smiling at someone you can sense needs a lift, or making dinner for a friend who is going through a hard time, or in creating a business like a day care or an animal rescue.

There are a hundred ways to live your purpose. Purpose is a part of you and everything you do; it is not only linked to our careers. Purpose is not the outcome of what we do, it is the way we live and how we impact those around us.

And yes, it should be the central part of your career and the way you make money. So, let's work through this equation together.

Your natural skills are things you have always been good at, have come naturally to you, or you've been told since you can remember are talents you hold. They can be anything from drawing to problem-solving to seeking justice to body movement. They really can be anything.

For me, my natural skills have always been intuitively seeing a solution to complex problems quickly. As an eight-year-old, I'd sit with my newly divorced mother as she'd talk to other family members and start to lose patience. After hearing hours of deliberation about some decision she needed to make, I'd chime in and say, "Here's what you need to do!"

They'd laugh it off, but every time I would do that, they would inevitably come back at some point and say, "You're going to grow up to be a therapist." (There was no word for "intuition coach" back then, so I guess I'll give them that one.)

When you are working at something that employs these natural skills, you tend to find more joy in that work. You know why? Because your natural talents are no accident. This too is an intelligent implant from Higher Self and the Universe, both of which want you to do something on this planet that creates positive impact for everyone on it. Your natural skills and talents are a part of you because they are meant to allow you to do your purpose with ease without feeling like an imposter or a fraud.

That feeling of ease in doing something you're good at creates joy and passion. These are feelings Higher Self wants for you. You are meant to enjoy the doing of your purpose, so you *want* to do it. It's a positive reward mechanism rather than a negative one that pushes you to be something you're not to get the validation of others. In this reward mechanism, doing the work that comes naturally to you feels good so that you can enjoy the doing of your purpose. The joy or the fulfillment is the internal validation that you're on the right track. That's the kind of validation that fills you up instead of draining you.

Finally, what is the impact part of the purpose equation? Here's where the myths created by old power structures in business come back into play. We are taught that we are in a zero-sum game, an either/or; either they succeed—or you do. We aren't taught an abundance mindset that says *both* can win. What if this conclusion is based on a fundamentally flawed premise?

The impact part of your purpose equation means that the work that comes naturally to you *and* provides you with fulfillment or joy will also create a positive impact on the community around you, however large or small. That's right—both you and those you are here to help can succeed simultaneously. You don't have to win at their expense, nor do you have to suffer in order to help others. That's a scarcity mindset. Your purpose, driven by your Higher Self, is never from a scarcity mindset. Your purpose is full of abundance and only understands abundance.

I know it is hard when you work for someone else to imagine how you might live your purpose while working for their dreams. The good news is that if you are honest about understanding your own purpose equation, you will get really good at seeing when your dreams overlap with another person's dreams. This is where it does become possible to be in your purpose, to be aligned with Higher Self, while working for others. You don't have to quit your job and start a business to achieve your purpose—or you can! You know who is waiting to guide you on that question, right?

Just promise me you won't be hard on yourself as you figure it out. Because here's the thing: No one taught you the purpose equation in school. No one made you stop and think through it as you applied for your first job. That's okay—it's all part of the learning. It's hard to really know what lights us up, to really understand our skills and the impact we want to make on the world, without just going out into the world and trying things.

Do I wish we had been taught to do this while also consulting with our own truth and desires along the way? Absolutely. But that doesn't change the learnings this process gave us. I'm not here to warn against learning about yourself in that way, by trying things on for size. That's a natural process and I love that for you. What I am here to remind you is that success without true inner fulfillment is not only not a win, it's not even the game.

If that resonates with you, then really pause and take the rest of this in. You may have the title, the money, or the power you always wanted, but something's missing. You're not happy with what you have achieved. That's okay. Your lack of satisfaction doesn't make you ungrateful or undeserving of your accomplishments. That void just means you're waking up. You're waking up to the truth that being aligned to your Higher Self is not the same as achieving a long list of material success, and it's not the same as having your ego feel good about who you are.

Being aligned to your Higher Self, you see, is not about outcomes at all. It is about a state of being. A feeling of centeredness in knowing that you're living in accordance with your own truth, with your values, and with the desires for this life you have, not anyone else's. Being aligned to Higher Self means you are living for you and for no one else.

Whatever comes from living this way are just natural outputs of a life well lived. You don't have to strive so hard to achieve your goals, you just have to get your inner world aligned, and naturally, your outer world will match. It's a law of nature: what is within will be reflected on the outside as long as you give it time to take root and grow.

EXPLORATION: *Diagnosing Purpose*

If you're feeling that void despite being in a job or career you strived for all your life, take a moment and do this exercise. This will help you give yourself a little more grace and clarity as you navigate the path back to your Higher Self.

Think about and write out your answers to the following prompts:

- What made you choose this career?
- What did you believe succeeding in this job or career would mean about you?
- What internal truth, desire, or personal values have you had to sacrifice to succeed in this job or career?
- What longings are you ignoring because of the fear that following them won't amount to material success?

PART III

# Becoming Reconnected

CHAPTER 9

# Making Room

*You're ready to listen—that's what* drew you to this book. It is no accident that you are here today reading these words. You have been feeling the absence of your Higher Self. Of course, you probably wouldn't have described it that way.

Maybe you just felt a restlessness you couldn't describe.

Maybe you were tired of feeling stuck or of reliving old pain.

Maybe you are ready for a change, and you know it is time to take the next step.

All of these feelings stem from the same desire: to reunite with that old friend, the wise expansive voice within. All of this is a sign that you are done playing small, conforming to what others expect, that you're ready to discover your truth and live it—finally.

*Welcome back*, Higher Self is saying, *I've been waiting for you.*

### Your Younger Selves Show Up to Speak Truth

To really hear what Higher Self has to say, we have to clear the pathway. To do that, we are going to go back to your limiting beliefs. This time, in addition to identifying them, we are going to give them a chance to speak to us, hear what they have to say, and give them a chance to meet your Higher Self. This process is more than healing your limiting beliefs. I call this process **reintegration.**

Remember that your limiting beliefs are just younger aspects of you that are still stuck in a thought or feeling that was designed to protect you from the pain you experienced in that moment. From now on, when you think of your limiting beliefs, I want you to think of them as you at different ages. If there's an aspect of you that believes the thought *We will never make that dream come true,* we are now going to look at that belief and ask, "How old are you?" When we see a seven- or thirteen- or seventeen-year-old show up in answer to that question, we are going to assign that belief to ourselves at that age. This is critical in the process of realigning with your Higher Self again.

These younger aspects of you are still working very hard to protect you by replaying these limiting beliefs.

And now, you've outgrown them. You aren't just looking to survive anymore. You are ready to thrive. This gives these belief systems, the marching orders of the younger aspects of you, a new, less stressful job. They don't need to work so hard to protect you. Instead, they only need to inform you about their needs. From there, you and Higher Self will get them, and you, everything they have ever wanted. After a lifetime of unknowingly marching to their orders, you are going to show up and rescue them from their misguided cause.

The work we do in this chapter will be slightly different from that in the preceding chapters. Really, the methodology below is an evolution of what you learned to practice in Chapter Three. Whereas previously you were practicing being able to recognize and listen to Higher Self in your present life, now we are going to get granular. With that newly established connection, we are going to bring Higher Self to our loud, demanding younger selves to reintegrate all those critical aspects of you into one whole self.

### Three Steps to Reintegration

The younger aspects within you who have designed limiting beliefs have been in charge for most of your life. I am willing to bet they are mostly in charge today. Since those beliefs worked so well to keep us safe, they have been rewarded with your increased belief in them. For example, if you feel anxious about trying something new and make the decision from that belief not to, you do remain safe. The younger aspect within that created that thought thinks: *Well done! I did what I'm here to do.* That's the reward right there—your safety. Mission accomplished.

That reward tells this younger aspect who holds this belief that your survival still depends on it, so it gets louder and louder. It takes its job very seriously. The process of reintegration is about interrupting the thought *To say safe, you better [fill in the blank].*

Interrupting the thought is done easily when you learn to take three steps:

1. Identify and Separate
2. Listen Without Judgment
3. Appreciate and Redirect

Let's get into detail on how to execute each of these steps below.

### STEP 1. IDENTIFY AND SEPARATE

Good news: by this point in the book, you have already had the chance to identify your limiting beliefs. If you need to remind yourself of them, no problem. Pull out that list from Chapter Three and spend a little time in reflection. Now we are going to take those limiting beliefs and try to assign this thought to a younger aspect of you. In order to uproot the belief, we need to know exactly which previous version of you is holding on to it.

Sometimes this is easier said than done. Sometimes these younger aspects of you have gotten so good at blending in and pretending to be you today that they don't immediately offer an age when you stop to do the internal exploration. Sometimes these younger aspects have also gotten so used to having their needs ignored that they don't quite trust you yet. They have learned that you only listen if they repeat the limiting belief they hold. They do not trust you to care about the needs they have deep down underneath the limiting beliefs.

Examples of this pattern can help. You've been ignoring *I want to feel loved*, but you do listen to *Say yes so this person will like you*. You do this because the first statement is too hard to address and too painful to face. The second prompt, *Say yes so this person will like you*, is very actionable and easy to do. When you succumb to people pleasing, you have unknowingly ignored the need in favor of the limiting belief.

The key here is to separate your current self as the one having the thought from the younger version of you that still holds the belief. When we confuse the limiting belief a younger version of us is still operating from with our current way of thinking, we are ignoring the younger self. The unlocking part of this step is to see the younger version as separate from the current version of you so you can give it the attention and love it's needing so badly.

I have an incredibly gifted client who works in the arts; he is critically acclaimed and has the industry awards to prove it. Despite this external validation, he believes he is lacking somehow, that something about the way he lives and makes decisions is flawed (lazy, even) despite all the success. He's quick to brush aside compliments and even quicker to find the flaws in his way of life. He believes that his success is more a result of how he motivates others to work with him rather than from the true genius that lives inside.

Immediately when meeting him I can see a younger boy behind these statements, a kid who originally heard these projections and believed them. When we do our visitations with this younger boy together, we close our eyes and I get us started. I navigate us through a visual of a forest, then a staircase, and down into a darker, more hidden space. Usually at this point my clients will take over, guiding us both down whatever path they are seeing unfold with their eyes closed.

On this day, we go down into a cavernous space filled with smaller, dark spaces made of rock juxtaposed with sunlight beaming through breaks in the cave walls above us. It's down here that we find him, seven or eight years old, surrounded by toys and cartoons, wanting so badly to just play. No big revelations. No emotional outburst. Just play. It took us weeks to even get the younger boy to speak, so we'd go down there and just play with him. This seemed to be what he wanted.

After a few sessions of visualizing this boy surrounded by his toys and drawings, paying attention to the pieces he wanted to show off, we finally heard it. It came through to my client like a thought in the middle of our visualization: *I'm not doing enough, I'm too childish.*

"Who's saying that?" I asked.

"The boy in the cave," he replied.

Now we had a dialogue. This was the opening we needed.

Someone, when he was very young, wanted more from him. They wanted him to try harder. They wanted him to do more, to be like the athletic kids who played on three different teams and succeeded at everything they tried. That wasn't him. He was a creative, sensitive, and incredibly intelligent boy who preferred to spend his hours imagining worlds and characters that unfolded into stories. He wasn't understood, so he took on the beliefs that the adults projected. He never knew that little boy was in there, still holding tight to those same beliefs, despite his turning those stories into award-winning art as an adult.

I want you to try this for yourself. Take a moment to do a visualization. Invite your younger self to speak. See with your mind's eye. When you repeat the limiting belief, who is saying it? More than likely, you will immediately know. The picture of yourself at a certain and specific age will occur to you. Take some time to observe yourself in this moment in time so you can identify which younger self is preaching beliefs that no longer serve you.

If your younger self isn't presenting so easily, don't worry. Since these younger selves have been ignored for so long, they aren't sure whether you mean it this time, so be patient. They'll eventually emerge as you do the work. Be patient with the little you that is yelling under the weight of some very heavy responsibilities.

You can begin to slowly coax it out by showing up every time you feel it activated within you and just giving it your loving attention. "Hey," you can say, "I see you're back and you're trying to protect me. What do you really need?"

What's the first response you get? Trust that this answer is coming from that younger version beneath who has just been triggered. Simply trusting the first answer you get can open a dialogue with this part of you.

Once you can identify which aspect of you holds the limiting belief, then you must separate your current self from that aspect. It is not present you who holds this belief that is limiting you from achieving your desires and purpose, it is a much younger self who is still stuck in a painful moment. Hold that distinction in your mind.

If you can do this, you are well on your way. This separation can be incredibly empowering to you. It creates limitless possibility within you. If you are not your limiting belief, then what are you capable of?

*Everything.*

### STEP 2. LISTEN WITHOUT JUDGMENT:

Once you have identified the younger-self origin of your limiting beliefs, it is time to listen to that aspect of yourself. If you can accept that this is a younger aspect of you still stuck in a moment of pain using an old strategy to try and protect you, then you can also see that this child within still has needs.

Those needs are very real. So real, in fact, they have been unconsciously guiding your decision-making all this time. You want to be the one steering your decisions through the powerful guidance of your intuition, your Higher Self, but you haven't been able to hear that wise intuitive voice fully because you haven't stopped to give this little one what it actually needs.

Have you ever seen a kid who wants something throw a temper tantrum? That is exactly what's happening inside when you ignore your younger self and their needs. This tantrum can manifest as so many things: anxiety, depression, fear, nonstop worry, and so on. Your younger self is talking to you nonstop through limiting beliefs, but you're only listening to those limiting beliefs while also confusing them with your own thoughts. Beneath those beliefs are needs. It is time to listen to the needs so that the little one within can let up and give your Higher Self some room to guide you.

So, what needs does younger self have? Your younger self is still operating from a moment in time where they were somehow hurt or disappointed. What is it they are wanting to help make that hurt or disappointment feel better? Your job, along with Higher Self, is to figure that out.

There are a few challenges here. First is that you may lack experience dealing with kids the age of the younger self who has shown up. Dealing with any age group requires a specific set of skills. I often tell my clients to picture a young child of the same age who is currently in their lives.

What questions would they ask that child who came to them about a disappointment?

How would they listen?

What would they say?

The second challenge is that your younger self might need to voice a truth that is difficult for you to hear. In fact, you know it's difficult; that's why you have been choosing to adhere to the limiting belief rather than healing the pain underneath it. Sometimes, I have noticed, my clients react to their younger selves not with empathy and love but with fear. They don't want to hear what their younger self has to say. They are afraid their younger self will look at their current self and wonder what it was all for.

This fear can show up in a lot of ways, most commonly in not being able to see a younger version of themselves at all. Or, sometimes, when we do find this younger self in our visualization, they won't be able to see their face or make eye contact with this inner child. When this happens, I know two things are going on: the person trying to communicate with their younger self fears some truth that self holds about them or feels shame toward this aspect of themselves. So of course, the younger self within will inherently distrust the connection and refuse to engage in the dialogue. Who wants to talk to someone who doesn't want to hear what they have to say or is ashamed of them?

That kind of fear and defensiveness is not the bedrock of great listening. But that's okay. There are work-arounds. First, grant yourself some compassion—and extend that to your younger self too. Your younger self holds a hard truth, but it isn't anything you don't already know. Now, as an adult, you will be much better equipped to deal with that need than when you were a child. Trust in that to help you keep an open mind.

In addition, your younger self, contrary to your present fears, is not angry with you. They will not be disappointed in who you have become. They will be thrilled to see you, thrilled that someone is listening. Trust that you have the tools to meet their need now, even though you didn't when you were small. You just need to invite them to speak the real need beneath the demand.

The key here is to listen *without judgment* to the needs. These needs usually fall into those same three human needs categories we talked about earlier: the need to belong, to be loved, and to have dignity.

Listening is about figuring out which of those needs went unmet for that younger version of you without judgment *or* making excuses for the people who were around at that time. It is normal, especially if these people are still in your life, to be tempted to interrupt the listening with the thought that defends those people: *Oh, Dad was just working really hard to provide for us* or *Mom did her best to be loving, but she didn't have loving parents who modeled that for her.*

Those things may very well be true, and I applaud you for your empathy, I really do. But when you interrupt younger self to give that perspective, what you're saying to that aspect of you is that their needs are less important than everyone else's needs. This is dangerous and self-defeating.

Your younger self *already believes* their needs are less important than everyone else's—that's why they've created beliefs that are still limiting you. They already believe they aren't enough; you don't need to remind them. Your job is to empower them for the first time by listening.

This will be the first experience this younger aspect of you may have had being listened to, trusted, and valued for their truth. Listen so that you can rebuild trust with younger self, so that this child within you knows their experiences matter and that you're finally here to show them that is true. That is the sad but beautiful irony of this entire dynamic. Your younger self has been crying out all while making its demands known in the most punishing way to the present you. That love your younger self was seeking has actually been available to it the entire time. *We* are who are younger selves have been waiting for.

### STEP 3. APPRECIATE AND REDIRECT

If you have really given the younger aspect within you a chance to tell you what it needs without judgment, it will *keep* telling you. This is a beautiful thing! This means that now the inner dialogue is about what you have actually needed all this time, rather than all the limitations or worries you've been spending your time listening to instead. Now that your younger aspect is speaking, you can do something about them.

Your needs, which have been accumulating as you've grown, must be met. There is no other way of achieving peace of mind so that you can move forward toward your dreams unencumbered. Once your younger self begin to tell you its needs, it is time to acknowledge that you have heard them.

However far people get with reintegration, I have heard all kinds of excuses for why this step is not worth the time.

Sometimes my clients will say to me, "I don't have the time to be in this conversation."

"Really?" I ask. "But you do have the time to listen to worries all day long?"

This process doesn't take more time than listening to your limiting beliefs. It is much more efficient once you practice it. This, just like listening to your worries and fears, is an inner dialogue but a productive and healing one, whereas giving attention to your limiting beliefs is draining and hopeless. Which would you choose?

This conversation is simple. As you listen to your younger self express a need, you just need to acknowledge that need. You can say something like "II hear you," or "I understand, I want that too." Just acknowledge. That's it.

Now what will happen is that younger self will try to get that need met by repeating the limiting belief. That could look like, "Okay, so to get that, let's just say *yes* to this project so people see we're valuable." It's not their fault. They've been stuck in this pattern so long, and it's worked (sort of) until now.

This is where you move into the last step: **appreciate and redirect.**

First, you want to appreciate your younger self for working so hard to protect you by bringing up a strategy it created long ago to help you survive.

Tell them, "Thank you for trying so hard to help and protect me."

That's it—just express gratitude. It's that simple.

Imagine a little kid who had to give up the joy of being a kid to protect you. How would you talk to them? You would be touched by this act, and you would be grateful that they love you so much they are willing to sacrifice their own joy to keep you safe. This what your younger self has been doing this whole time. *Thank you*, younger self! That is a big sacrifice.

Then, redirect them: "Thank you for trying to protect me, but we're trying a different way now that we are safe. All you need to do now is tell me what you need, that's your only job."

You can even give them the homework of giving you evidence. The fear they're projecting is asking you to take action in a way they believe is best, but stop and ask them, "Do we have any evidence that doing it that way actually gets us what we need?" The answer is usually no, there is no evidence, because if their strategy worked, they wouldn't still be trapped in fear. Now that it's clear their strategy hasn't worked, you get to ask if they're willing to try it a new way.

This is a new purpose for these aspects of you that have been working so hard on your behalf this whole time. Give them a new reason to exist that doesn't include projecting their limiting beliefs, which—reminder—have been projected onto them by others. Their only job now is to tell you what they need and to trust that you are going to go get it. Their needs are your needs, and you're on a journey now to hear those needs and understand that you deserve to have them met.

Isn't that beautiful?

Not only do you deserve to have those needs met, you have been put here with an important purpose, so you *need* to have them met. Without getting your needs met, you can't live your purpose! Your purpose is a part of who you are and has been ingrained in you to help you grow and help others. What sense would it make for you to be put here with such an important mission and then not be able to accomplish it because your own needs haven't been met?

To create any impact in the world and on your own life, you have to start by getting what you need. I am saying this both to you today and also to younger you. I want you to let your younger self know this too. Their needs are everything. Let them flow. You are here to get them all met and more.

### Reintegration Exercise

This work is a consistent dialogue that must happen every time you hear a limiting belief from within. Whatever that limiting thought is, I want you to stop and have the inner dialogue I just walked you through. The more you do this, the more natural it becomes and the faster it can happen each time.

Let's do this together now. You may want to read through the exercise below first and then try it with your eyes closed or follow along as you are ready. Whichever way feels right to you.

### STEP 1. IDENTIFY AND SEPARATE

Where are you currently holding yourself back in life? What belief do you hold that tells you you can't have what you want?

How long have you held this belief? Close your eyes and ask, "How old are you?" You may get an age here, which you should note, or you might not, and that's okay. Keep doing the rest of the exercise and eventually it will come to you, if not in this instance, in the next or the one after that. Your younger self will see that you keep showing up, trying to find and give it what it needs. It will show up eventually even if it doesn't right away. Just be patient.

Now stop, and in your mind separate the belief from the younger aspect. See the belief as a protective shield and ask it to step aside. You can even say to yourself or out loud: "I see you there trying to protect me. Can you step aside so I can figure out what I need?"

### STEP 2. LISTEN WITHOUT JUDGMENT

Take a look at your younger self. What does it really need? What was it missing at that point in time? What would have made it feel good? Happier? Safer?

Listen.

Maybe it's saying, *I want to feel like I matter*, or, *I want to feel loved*. Whatever you hear, take it seriously. Know this: you in the current moment are the loving guide, mentor, and parent your younger self has been waiting for all this time. Take on that loving parental or mentor tone as you think about this next part. Don't make excuses for why they didn't get what they needed. Just listen and relate.

### STEP 3. APPRECIATE AND REDIRECT

Look that younger part of you in the eye and tell them at least three reasons why they are whatever they are needing to feel.

Make those reasons meaningful. Tell them, for example, that they are lovable, important, special, and valuable. Really think about it. What was it about you at that age that did make you so spectacular? Were you funny, free-spirited, curious, or focused? Were you energetic, creative, and kind? Whatever words come to mind, tell your younger self exactly who you see from this vantage point.

Now appreciate this aspect of you for working so hard all this time to protect you. Express your gratitude at the hard work they have done. Then, redirect them. Remind this aspect that all they need to do from now on is tell you what they need, then you and Higher Self will go get those needs met. But you will do so in a new way—no longer with the outdated strategy of limiting beliefs they are presenting but in an intuitive and empowered way that says: *Everything we want is within us. It is all possible.*

Take some deep breaths and let it all sink in.

Here is the truth: your fear voice, these younger parts of you, are just there to be witnessed, not followed. Learning to embody your inner wisdom in a centered way will happen when you understand that your job is to listen to the aspects of your younger self and their needs, not follow their guidance. Guidance should come only from your Higher Self. Fear selves = listening; Higher Self = action.

### An Everyday Practice

The exercise you just learned is meant to be a tool you utilize several times throughout your day. Any time, in fact, you feel a limiting belief pop up that is holding you back, you can initiate this dialogue. At first, it may take you some time, but as you keep having the inner dialogue, the entire process will speed up and become a natural part of the way you think.

That's what we're doing here: rewiring the way your brain processes the information you get. Before, when a limiting belief popped in, your brain was trained to take it as fact and operate with that fact as its compass. Now we see that these beliefs are far from factual. Instead, these are limiting ideas created by your younger self as a means to survive. Your brain has an opportunity to create a new pathway, one that questions the limiting belief and learns to identify the needs beneath it.

My most powerful limiting belief was created by an eight-year-old version of myself. After those long years of infidelity, my parents finally decided to divorce. My mom, sister, and I picked up and moved from Colorado to Maryland, where my mom had family, while my dad went in a different direction. My mom, who had only worked as a seamstress in the US, was on her own, raising two kids in a new state.

To say money was tight is a massive understatement. Initially, we moved into a three-bedroom townhouse with my uncle and his family where eight people tried to squeeze into a space that would have been moderately comfortable for a family of four.

My mom and I shared a bedroom. At night, when she thought I was asleep, I'd hear her quietly crying next to me in the bed, trying hard to graft together what was left of her heart. In the mornings, she'd put on a cheery face, like she had always done, crack some jokes, and set out to find a job.

"Everything is great!" she'd say, as I'd notice her swollen, red eyes.

It wasn't easy. She worked as a seamstress at JCPenney until she found office work for the federal government. Regardless, money was still tight, and her heart was still broken. I remember looking at her face when we had to go grocery shopping, watching the lines on her forehead strain as she worked out how many times she would have to say no to me when I asked for brand-name cereal or some snack I saw on TV.

I watched her balance and rebalance her checkbook when her part of the mortgage was due or when I had a school field trip she needed to pay for. I watched her struggle to figure out how to take over the mortgage of that house once my uncle and his family were ready to move out, taking on extra jobs to do at home once she came home from her twelve-hour days. I watched, but she didn't know how closely I was paying attention.

Here's the thing about my mom: ever since I can remember, when the shit hit the fan, my mom would put on loud Persian music and make my sister and me dance with her. She'd make us dance until the laughter and joy of that movement made us forget why were sad to begin with. That is how much she tried to change the impact of this moment in my life, to try and make sure I never had to tell this story.

And yet, with all that effort on her part, the thing that stuck out the most to eight-year-old me was the belief that there would never be enough money to keep me safe from being brokenhearted. I conflated my mother's broken heart and disappointment in the ending of her marriage with the stress I saw on her face when she tried to provide for us. Any lack of money equated to a broken heart to me. It did then, and my eight-year-old tries very hard to convince me of the same today.

I use this exercise at least four times a week because eight-year-old me is still so convinced she must protect me by reminding me that money can crush me one day. If a client I'm working with decides, very naturally, to stop working with me, or a bill comes that I don't expect, or my husband seems stressed as he balances our budget, my eight-year-old pops her little head up: *Here it comes! We're doomed! DOOOO something!*

I've learned to stop the thought right there. "What's the limiting belief here?" I'll ask myself.

*It's that money will go away, and I will be brokenhearted,* I get in answer.

I've done this enough not to have to ask how old this belief is. I know it's her, so I'll say in my head, "There you are! I see you." I say this with love, like I would have to my own daughter when she was eight and would come home from school.

Then I'll ask her, "What do you really need right now?"

The answer changes, but usually it's something like, *To not have to worry about being sad because we have no money so I can just go play.* (We love fun, her and I.)

There's the need: not to have to worry and to be able to enjoy life. Now I have the information I need from her to get her need met for her, and for me. I don't need the limiting belief about money to get that need met. All I need is for her to tell me what she needs. The rest is up to me and Higher Self.

We take a break from the stressor so that it doesn't continue to build up. I like to spend time outside—usually at the beach walking along the surf. That's where I can remember my joy. And then I'm ready to engage with my Higher Self, who can remind me that while the fear is not having enough money, I'm remembering it through the lens of my much younger self . . . and that's not who I am anymore.

This dialogue with my younger self is only possible because I'm taking care of eight-year-old me, not letting her take care of us. By the time I come back home, the fear and worry about money has dissipated. It may take some rebalancing of the budget, sure, or there may be struggles ahead, but I can recognize the root of the fear and work with that—and I've soothed that inner voice, the younger self, worrying that everything will disappear.

She got her needs met and I can move forward without being weighed down by such an old worry. Here we are, alive in the present, soothed and reassured, no longer imprisoned by the wounds of the past.

EXPLORATION: *Checking In*

Learning to do this organically and in the moment takes practice. As you go into your day-to-day, I'd like you to try this exercise:

When you feel yourself reacting with emotion to anything, big or small, try stopping and identifying who is having that big emotion and see if you can start a quick and easeful dialogue.

Some helpful prompts as you talk to younger you:

# Making Room

I see you there. What's wrong right now? What are you afraid of?

Instead of telling me what we should do, can you tell me what you need?

What if I try to get those needs met in a new way? Can you trust me to try?

Thanks for trying to protect me. You don't have to work so hard anymore. I've got you.

CHAPTER 10

# Learning the Language of Your Soul

It took you a long *while to come back to yourself, but here you are.*
You feel the pull from somewhere deep inside, the familiar voice calling out:

*It's time to come back home.*

You know it's the only way to thrive, to finally let out a deep breath and with it, unfold everything you have held in so tightly to fully emerge in your truth.

*Welcome back, my love. I've been waiting,* your Higher Self whispers.

In this chapter, you will learn to recognize the patterns and presence of your own intuitive voice.

On that evening while I sat on the floor of our kitchen, twenty-nine years old, eight months pregnant with my son, married to my first husband, I heard the call, and I, for the first time in a very long time, decided to believe in this part of me again.

I decided to believe that I was full of wisdom and truth, that I had the grit, resilience, and love within me to navigate something I knew would be heartbreaking. I took that leap because I finally believed my Higher Self when she told me there was something much more aligned to my truth on the other side of it.

Coming back into the understanding that she and I were the same, that I could embody all that clarity and honesty, has been the greatest love story of my life. To know that this aspect of me never left me behind, never grew impatient with my many attempts at getting love and validation from the outside, and never judged my inner children who ran around doing anything for safety, even if it meant existing outside the dignity she so steadily provided.

Once I remembered who I was, that she was me and I her, it felt simply like coming back home. Like slipping underneath an old blanket that conformed to my body and surrounded me with all the love and security I had been looking for in others. The reunion with my Higher Self was for me an awakening to the fact that I was never alone, even in my loneliest moments. It was a reminder that all my greatest triumphs had her whispers behind them, and all my failures were a pathway back to her overwhelming love and support.

### Unconditional Love Is Waiting

*If you believe it, then it's true.* This statement doesn't only apply to limiting beliefs, it applies to your Higher Self too. Thus far, your wise guide has been waiting patiently as you experience the smallness of a life built in the image of other people's version of the truth. It watched as you strove for their attention, praise, and love. It watched lovingly as you, in pursuing those things, made every effort possible to suppress its soulful guidance.

Maybe, if this were a more human aspect, it would be frustrated with you. Maybe it would be hurt that you forgot it existed, or even worse, you knew it was there and ignored it purposefully, diligently. Maybe if this were a more human aspect, it would want to punish you somehow for trading it in for the acceptance of others. Maybe it would want to make you work hard to earn back its loving guidance once again. It might make you repent and promise to never abandon it again or hold out on you until you somehow proved you were worthy of its love.

But it doesn't feel any of those things. It isn't angry with you, or disappointed or judgmental over your choices. Why? Because your Higher Self is composed of one thing and one thing only: **unconditional love.** This whole time as you have been trying hard to ignore your truth to gain love and acceptance, it has been loving you through it, loving you enough to let you take the longer, more winding road, knowing that each and every experience of journeying further from yourself would only bring you back more fully to yourself when you were ready.

But now, you have made room. You have looked at your limiting beliefs and begun to give them the love and acceptance they have been waiting so long for. In doing that, you've allowed them to quiet down, to settle and find peace. This peace you have created and will continue to create by using these practices is not only good for your mind and body, but it is also essential for your soul.

You have now created room for your soul to speak to you once again. You have made space for Higher Self to make itself heard. The work you have done and will continue to do to address your limiting beliefs head-on has provided the perfect stage for your Higher Self to reemerge. You are ready now to meet it again, to listen and to trust it. It is time to learn how to recognize it again. Here you are, ready to get reacquainted, and your Higher Self is delighted to see you. But first you need to remember what its communication to you feels and sounds like.

*Welcome back, my love. I've been waiting.*

Read those last few words again and then close your eyes. What thoughts and feelings arise in you as you remember the very core of who you are, this magical, endless, knowing aspect of you?

Make note of these thoughts, feelings, and sensations. These are good reminders and clues to look for as you go about your day-to-day. Knowing what your Higher Self feels like when it shows up is so critical to learning to pay attention to it. Remember that your Higher Self speaks to you through *intuition*. Intuition is the language of your Higher Self. To help you understand that it is present, it gives you signals so that you can recognize and pay attention to its presence and what it is here to say.

There is no one signal that is common to all people. Your Higher Self and its language of intuition is unique to you. It requires curiosity and exploration. It asks that you be more curious and excited about getting to know yourself than you have been to understand anyone else. To help you in this exploration, I am going to break down for you the three common areas where intuition speaks up: in your **body,** in your **energy,** and in your **emotions**. Exploring these three areas in depth will help you to better understand how your Higher Self communicates to you.

### In the Body

"Right in the pit of my stomach!" my client tells me during a session when I ask him to close his eyes and pinpoint where the knowing voice inside is coming from.

"Great," I say. "Put both of your hands there and keep your eyes closed. What's the first thing it wants you to know?"

He pauses a moment, takes in a deep breath, and smiles. Before he responds to me, he lingers in whatever feeling is creating this beautiful smile across his face and we sit there in silence.

This is the best part of any session for me, when my clients finally hear their Higher Self so clearly, when I can tell that they are communicating without my help. At that point my job is to get out of the way and allow the reunion to unfold. After a while my client begins to relay what he's hearing from this inner wisdom, slowly and tentatively at first, then with more excitement and assuredness.

"Well, the first thing I heard is, *You're safe*, and then, *You're not alone, I've got you,*" he says.

My client, a well-known actor, and I have been working on a reoccurring fear he's been having about an upcoming role he's set to play. Something about this role set him off and sent him plunging back into the limiting beliefs of his childhood that told him no one cares what he has to say, to just stay quiet and out of the way so he doesn't get humiliated at school again.

It took us weeks of working with this younger aspect, of sitting with that younger self in our mind's eyes in that school cafeteria or on the stage of a school assembly where he was openly mocked during a talent show. We sat and we listened to this younger version of him tell us all his fears. We learned to recognize his little self every time he showed up, so that instead of listening to the limiting beliefs he projected, we listened to his needs. By doing this consistent work, this younger aspect had begun to let up in the past few weeks. I knew it was time. The peace the younger self was allowing would make room for my client to reunite with his inner power and meet his Higher Self once again.

"Beautiful," I say when he tells me that Higher Self has instilled a powerful reminder about him being safe. "What's it saying to you now?" I ask.

The smile returns to his face. Sitting there, looking more serene than I had ever seen him before, he says slowly, "That my gift is here to help more people than just me. That by performing I'm allowing others to see themselves in my characters, in my stories. That I make people feel seen."

Powerful reminders from this wise source.

"What does your Higher Self want you to do with that reminder?" I ask.

"Know that the craving for safety when I was younger is present in so many people and it is okay to go back to that feeling for this role because it will help others feel hopeful."

Your Higher Self is here to communicate your purpose to you as it did with my client that day. Knowing that the obstacle in the way of his success in this role was a much younger aspect, his Higher Self showed up to help him realize that those experiences had a purpose and so do his gifts. From this more purposeful place, my client was able to tackle something that terrified him.

To this day, when I ask him what his inner wisdom has to say, he automatically puts his hand on his stomach as if by default. For him, this is where his intuition physically signals.

This is one way intuition can let you know it is speaking to you; by showing up in your body. Some of my clients say they feel it in their fingertips or as a flutter in their heart. Others describe it as a sense of expansion, as if they suddenly take up more space when they tune in and hear intuition. There are as many ways for intuition to show up in the body as there are people. That's why I can't tell you exactly where to look. The only way for you to know is to begin to pay attention and explore.

I feel my intuition in the pit of my stomach as if butterflies are fluttering, and also as a tingle at the very top of my head. Usually, the butterfly feeling comes when there is good news ahead that I wasn't expecting. I'll get that feeling and know something positive is coming, either for me or for someone I love. The tingling at the top of my head usually has more to do with information I am getting that will guide an important decision. This is also the feeling I get when in session with my clients when I start to receive important information for them. This, I realized years later, was the sensation I'd get back in my agency days when I was helping big companies make critical, game-changing decisions.

Learning to recognize these signals and differentiate between their meaning has been so empowering. Just by paying attention to the sensations occurring within my body, I was able to notice that there were two very different signals in different parts. Just noticing— that's where it all starts. This of course takes time. But the more I paid attention, the stronger the feelings would feel and I would learn, just through noticing their arrival, what to do with them.

In my work today helping others heal their limiting beliefs and find their Higher Self, I work with these signals nonstop. When I walk out of a session and tend to my own life, distinguishing these signals in my body helps me understand the difference between worry and anxiety and an intuitive knowing. This differentiation has been a lifesaver for a person like me who's lived with anxiety her whole life. My body lets me know when anxiety is speaking, and I know then that my job is to just stop and listen to the younger self who is projecting her worries. Similarly, my body tells me when the thoughts that are coming in are intuitive, and those are the thoughts I choose to act on.

It's your turn to explore this in your own physical self. When you have a thought that feels true, like *fact*, that comes out of nowhere, do you get a sensation in your body? Do you remember intuitive movements in the past and feeling those in your body? Make note of what comes up as you reflect. You can even ask Higher Self right now. Try it. Say, "Higher Self, can you show me where you show up in my body when you're speaking to me through my intuition?" Get anything? If you do, excellent, make note of it. If you don't, that is also okay. You are in good company.

My cousin Anais, who is basically like my younger sister, is an incredibly powerful medium. Ever since she was a baby, she could see or receive always spot-on information from spirits. She would tell us at the age of five or six years old that something was going to happen before it did. Once, at the age of eight, she had a premonition or visitation from a cousin who lived across the country. She woke up to run and tell her mom something was wrong with him only to find out he has been brutally murdered the night before.

As you can probably guess, this gift wasn't an easy burden to bear for her. It caused her a lot of pain and confusion in her life. That didn't stop her, though. She kept running toward it. She fearlessly leapt into an aspect of herself people told her was crazy because she wanted to know herself. Even more incredible, she did it because she always knew she was here to help others.

She is incredible. She's the person my sister and I go to when we want the most honest and clarifying insights. Not to mention, she somehow got the job of being the one who reminds me of who I am the most consistently. She sees multiple realms and holds them all with this infectious, buoyant joy and with so much love.

She says she wants to come back in the next life as a stand-up comedian. Sometimes I think she believes she is one in this lifetime. But no—in this lifetime she has to settle for simply being magical. Intuition is an obvious language to her, and yet, when I talk about feeling intuition in the body she always tells me there's either something wrong with what I'm saying or there's something wrong with her.

Actually, it is neither.

There are many reasons why you might not feel intuition in your body. One is that it may come through stronger in other areas, not needing to necessarily create a physical signal because it knows you receive it so clearly without one (which, by the way, is what I believe is true for my cousin).

For example, you may just have very distinct thoughts that you recognize as intuition, and therefore skip the part where your body has to give you a sign. Or, you may know that you always hear your intuition when you're sitting alone in silence in a certain setting, so it will drop in clearly in that moment without needing to connect through your body.

The second most common reason I see is related to past trauma that has to do with the body. Anytime we face trauma that's related to our physical body, it is possible to become disembodied—disconnected from the sensations of your body. Anything from physical harm, abuse, or sexual assault to bullying or self-harm from the past may create a disconnect from your body in your current state. This is your body's survival response to having experienced something very bad.[1]

If that feels true for you, introducing somatic healing is a great way to heal your body from its past trauma. Somatics is the practice of helping your body recognize where trauma resides within and provides tools to help release that trauma and heal those experiences. If you find the right coach, it is a beautiful tool that helps unlock so much sadness and so much potential. It is a strategy I have used as I have come into my own purpose, and I couldn't recommend it more.

Through this practice, I've learned that the work I do to help people hear the voice of their fear selves and distinguish it from their Higher Self is also mirrored in the body. This practice has really taught me how to literally feel my feelings. My somatic coach has taught me how to describe the feeling of anxiety in my body—heavy, like an elephant sitting on my chest with no room for air to escape; or fear—a tangled knot in my stomach that feels like it slithers and grows as it moves.

This ability to literally feel my feelings allows me to witness them, just like I teach my clients to witness their younger selves. In witnessing, the feelings are allowed to flow and ultimately dissipate. The body holds all of this, I have learned, and now I teach my clients how to connect the dots between these younger selves and where they reside in our bodies and Higher Self, and where those signals light up in us.

### The Somatic Practice of Blending

Here is a quick somatic exercise written for you by my sister and somatic coach, Mojgan Besharat:

In a somatic practice we call **blending,** we intentionally focus our attention inward to various parts of our body where we typically hold tension. These areas are our "armoring bands." They consist of our eyes, jaw, chest, shoulders, upper and lower back, our knees, and even our toes.

By bringing our focus and attention to the sensations that live in these parts, we can tune into all the pressure and emotions we hold in these parts. Blending with this reality means bringing compassion and acknowledging the hard work these parts of our body are doing for our survival. Blending with our survival strategies allows us to soften and open to choice.

1. Start by scanning your body for any areas you're experiencing discomfort, contraction, or tightening. Start with your eyes and simply notice any sensation as you move down your face into your shoulders, chest, arms, back, legs, and feet. As you are

scanning with your mind, allow your breath to guide you through your body.

2. Take a moment to notice what is happening internally in your body. Where do you feel this contraction? What are its qualities? Is it hard and sharp or numb and frozen? What other sensations are here (i.e., warm, cold, tingling, tight, heavy, etc.)? Typically, the more you can feel into this part of your body, the more information it will reveal to you. We are not trying to change anything here, we are simply noticing and recognizing without any judgment.

3. You can focus your attention on one area that you experience more contraction. Now ask this part of your body, "What do you want me to know about how you are taking care of me?" You might receive an answer in the form of a thought or a feeling that could sound something like I'm protecting you. Or you may notice emotion arising. Whatever it is, just take a minute to listen with curiosity, almost as if you are listening to a loved one sharing their experience of hardship. Sometimes, we are looking for dramatic expression or an epiphany. However, in this practice, we are slowing down to listen with an open mind to our body. We are quieting down to notice the subtleties of all the expressions that live inside us.

4. Recognize that your survival has depended on this part of your body being vigilant for your whole life. By acknowledging that there is tension or pain, numbness, or some form of contraction, you are honoring all the hard work these parts of your body have been doing to make sure you are safe, that you matter, and/or that you belong. You are not judging or trying to change anything here. When you honor all of the hard work your body has been doing for the sake of your survival, you are blending and being with all that it is holding.

5. Ask this part of you how it would like to be acknowledged. It may come to you as a movement of the arms or legs. It may be that you embrace yourself in a tight hug and breathe in the care you are giving yourself as you place a hand on your heart. For some of us, it may simply be wrapping ourselves in a nice blanket,

allowing these tense parts to melt and ease open, How does it want you to honor it? What would it like you to say to it or how would it like you to hold it?

As you do this exercise, the more you practice being with, without denying or trying to change, the sensations, emotions, and feelings that arise, the more you are bringing compassion and care to these parts of your body that hold contraction.

This is the essence of a blend practice. We are essentially accepting the existence of all the sensations and feelings that are currently present in our bodies. We are appreciating and recognizing the hard work of holding tension. As we do this, we may notice a very subtle softening of the contraction.

In somatics, we call this subtle shift from a place of contraction to a softening, an opening. An opening, like coming into an open field after being in a tight rugged valley, brings more possibility and choice in how we respond to life. Blend with the part of your body that is holding this contraction.

It may be difficult to locate intuition in your body because you just haven't had enough practice learning to check in. The same way we can be taught to ignore our inner wisdom, we are often taught to ignore our bodies when they speak to us. My hope is my sister's practice gives you a practical way back into conversation with your body.

This is important because many of us have been gaslit around the information we're receiving. Have you or a friend ever been told by a doctor, for example, that the pain or discomfort you're feeling isn't really happening? This happens to certain groups of people more than others, unfortunately. In working with clients from every background imaginable, I have noticed that this form of gaslighting happens most often with women, people of color, and those who are overweight.

That kind of treatment has severe negative impacts. People in those groups develop a fear of medical attention because often we are told by medical experts and authorities that the way our body is speaking to us is somehow wrong or being misinterpreted. Overweight people are often turned away by doctors for legitimate and sometimes life-threatening illnesses. Rather than running the proper tests, their doctor will immediately ask them to lose weight.

For women, having our bodies policed by those in authority has created a long-running mistrust of how it speaks to us. We believe somehow that our bodies are the property of someone else, so we do not listen to our bodies. What's worse, most medical research to date is done on men, so very little is known about how our bodies work compared to our male counterparts'. We have to exist in the mystery of it instead of receiving education and clarity.

For people of color, medical treatment has long been tainted with deep racism, whether that be cases of experimentation with dangerous medical treatments on bodies of color or outright ignoring people of color when they complain of illness.

This is such an unfortunate outcome of deeply ingrained systems of hierarchy and oppression. For many of us, feeling in charge of and empowered enough to trust our bodies is simply a privilege we have never been afforded. Finding intuition in our bodies becomes almost impossible. Don't despair. Your Higher Self is not deterred that easily, nor is it going to allow any form of oppression to keep it from guiding you toward your highest good. If you are still journeying toward that connection with your body, your Higher Self has other channels to get your attention.

If you fall into one of these categories, pay special attention to the other two methods for detecting intuition but also take a moment now to acknowledge that lacking trust in yourself isn't your fault; it's the result of trying to operate in a world that's telling you that you shouldn't exist as you are. Pay attention to when the temptation not to trust your body or your thoughts comes up and use this awareness to cut the cord. You don't have to accept those projections any longer.

Your empowerment rests in this rebellion right here. Refuse to accept that trusting yourself is dangerous. Speak up. If any part of your body is telling you something, listen to it. Step out of the power dynamic with others and speak up for your body, for yourself. It is your responsibility and it's exactly what your Higher Self wants you to do.

## In Your Energy

The second way that intuition shows itself to you is through your *energy*. When your Higher Self speaks to you through the language of intuition, it sends with it an energetic charge. As with the body, this energetic charge can feel different from one person to another. In some people the energy signature of intuition is exciting or uplifting. In others, it can be deeply calming and centering. However, unlike how individual bodies manifest intuition, there are some clear absolutes when it comes to intuition and your energy.

For starters, **intuition, when it shows up, is never draining**. This is such an important truth. An intuitive thought, whispered to you by your Higher Self, will never leave you feeling energetically depleted, exhausted, or overwhelmed. Intuition is not and never will be draining. It can be profound, powerful, and moving, but never at a cost. Second, intuition will either create an energy of excitement *or* calmness. It is always either one or the other. Your energy when receiving an intuitive thought will either be incredibly calm or very excited, and this can depend on the information you are getting.

When I am in the middle of helping someone navigate a crisis, my intuition is deeply calming. There is chaos going on around me, people are hurting, and there is an immediacy to the situation that requires quick action on my part. All of this suggests a frenetic energy driving quick action.

Yet, when I check in with Higher Self for guidance, the wisdom I receive that many clients come to me for comes through with deep calm. I don't feel drained, regardless of the weight of the crisis, because my intuition is guiding me to help others in a very steady-handed and calm way. This energy then comes through in the way I provide guidance, allowing me to channel my calmness to people who are in a state of anxiety and fear.

On the flip side, when the information you are receiving is good news, giving you a sneak peek into an exciting future event, the energetic signature that comes along with that information is also exciting. You will notice that you feel like you literally have more energy. Maybe you are quicker to laugh or smile than usual, or you might notice you're feeling hyper, like you had one more cup of coffee than usual. There's a buzzed feeling that can come for some people in receiving intuitive information like this, which is an added bonus! Your Higher Self wants you to be excited about the good things coming to you. *Notice!* It says. *It is time to celebrate.* But that can be threatening to others.

That's the thing: sometimes our gifts scare other people. Everyone shows up with their own wounds, and it means that, sometimes, we aren't able to understand—or see—each other in our fullness. Sometimes it's a matter of parents trying to protect their children from something that harmed *them* during their own childhoods. Sometimes gifts are rejected simply because other people don't understand our gifts. They believe they have to protect us from them. But when you develop the confidence to see your gifts for what they are, it makes it *much* harder for someone to separate them from you.

Think now of your old friend, your intuitive voice. How do you feel energetically when you have a knowing feeling about something? In a fight or when faced with crisis, do you ever feel yourself becoming incredibly calm? Before something great happened to you—maybe you were considering a job change or just starting to date again or about to take on a new project—were you struck by a buzz of excited energy? If so, your Higher Self is speaking via those energetic forces. You just didn't know what to call it until now.

I still want to remind you of that nuanced but incredibly important distinction between energy that comes from your Higher Self . . . and energy that might share certain characteristics but doesn't. Are you ever exhausted or drained by the thought you are having, even if it comes with an energetic burst? If so, that isn't your intuition—those are your limiting beliefs creating fear and anxiety.

Practice working with your Higher Self to differentiate between the two. Ask a question and pay attention to the answer. When the answer creates a sense of calm or excitement, mark that in the intuition column. When you feel exhausted or drained, you know that's fear trying to protect you. Exhaustion is not the same thing as calm, and frenetic, draining energy is not the same thing as excitement. Knowing the difference is critical in recognizing Higher Self's voice.

### In Your Emotions

Your intuition is emotionally neutral. I'll say it again because it is *very* important: **your intuition is emotionally neutral.** This means that your Higher Self states things through your intuition very clearly and factually. There is no sadness, anger, frustration, anxiety, or fear in an intuitive thought or feeling. It is simply a *knowing*. Neutral. Even when your Higher Self is guiding you through something very difficult, or helping you make a difficult decision, it will state the information factually to you.

How do you know the difference? I have an easy test to distinguish between a fear thought/limiting belief and your Higher Self speaking. Here is what you do: If you have a thought or feeling that creates a difficult emotion, you now know immediately that this is not your intuition speaking. On the other hand, if you get a thought or feeling that comes through calmly and factually, like the period at the end of a sentence, you now know that is your intuition. Even a difficult truth will be communicated this way.

Remember me sitting on the kitchen floor, extremely pregnant with my second child, sobbing and desperate at the state of my marriage? The moment the thought occurred to me, *It's time to move on*, my crying ceased. The information I was getting was extremely difficult—that it was time to leave my marriage—and yet the way it came through was so clear, factual, and calm it made an incredibly painful situation feel almost empowering. And it felt empowering because after so much strife and uncertainty, I finally felt like I had a path forward.

Now, just because intuition is emotionally neutral doesn't mean your human self, filled with decades of limiting beliefs, will always react to the information without emotion. While the initial thought or feeling will be emotionally neutral, your younger aspects will immediately pop up to process the information alongside you. Those are the aspects that are still stuck in pain, fear, and anxiety, so they will of course react to the thought or feeling with pain, fear, or anxiety. That's their job. Remember your job is to hear their fears, find their deeper need, and console them. The better you can recognize your limiting beliefs and understand when they're surfacing, the better you'll be able to discern when your intuition is trying to reach you.

Knowing whether they are being spoken to by a fear or intuition, their younger self or their Higher Self, has been an incredibly powerful tool for my clients. Once you know which aspect of you is speaking, you are now in *choice*. You get to decide which aspect you will listen to. Even if you haven't quite untangled how to soothe your little selves, just knowing that there are both versions of yourself at work and learning how to recognize and distinguish between each will go a very long way.

Don't forget what to do when the fear voice pops up: identify which aspect of you is having the fear, separate your current self from that younger aspect, and then listen without judgment to what that younger self needs. As you do this, go back to the original thought that came in with neutrality.

1. Identify the source of the fear voice.
2. Separate your current self from your younger self.

3. Listen without judgment to your younger self's needs.
4. Ask Higher Self to repeat its message.

All of this said, I do want to acknowledge that there are conditions many of us live and struggle with that can make this process of listening to and trusting the intuitive voice even harder. For me, that's anxiety. Today, the three most common mental illnesses in the United States are anxiety, depression, and bipolar disorder. How do these conditions affect our relationship to hearing and trusting our intuition? I can only answer this question from my own experience with anxiety and from trying to help my clients who live with conditions like this access their intuition. To be clear, what you're about to read is not a medical or psychiatric opinion.

From my perspective, these conditions are outcrops of the same fears and limiting beliefs we've been talking about so far. Remember how I said our fear selves are younger, more vulnerable parts of us and that to protect these parts our limiting beliefs stand as bodyguards, projecting thoughts to protect us? In my experience, anxiety is one of these bodyguards. It's a constant running conveyor belt of different worries that arrive one after another to try and prepare me for some inevitable doom.

My anxiety believes that by doing this, I will be safe when that moment arrives, because I will know that it's coming. The problem, or miracle rather, is that the doom rarely ever arrives. Instead, I suffer through life, waiting for the sky to fall. Existing this way is so much worse than the temporary moments of crisis that crops up here and there in my life. When something painful happens, I find that I snap into action mode and deal with it. It's never the end of me, like my anxiety would have me believe. For me, this is how anxiety creates noise that blocks my intuition.

Still, I've found that using these three methods of identifying intuition in my body, energy, and emotions has at the very least helped me differentiate between what anxiety is saying and how it feels and how intuition shows up. It's tough to do, and takes a lot of practice, but in a moment of heightened emotions—when I'd usually notice my anxiety revving up—I try to press pause and identify the feeling. Is it a *real*, imminent threat, or is it my anxiety trying to protect me? Usually, it's the anxiety. From there, I talk to my anxiety the same way I'm telling you to talk to your fear self. I ask it what it's actually trying to take care of for me and through the act of having this dialogue, it lets up a little, and lets intuition break through clearly.

Depression is slightly different from anxiety. For much of my life, I've also struggled with seasonal and situational depression. Beyond the seasonal effect that the lack of light and warmth has on my mood, I've noticed that for me and some of my clients, depression is actually repression. When I refuse to feel my feelings or address something that's desperately needing my attention, depression will arrive and numb me.

Avoidance can be more comfortable than allowing yourself to full experience big feelings of fear, anger, or uncertainty. When I find myself in a period of depression, I've tried to practice doing just that. Even though it's incredibly difficult, I try to patiently let the waves of grief, anger or sadness roll over me. As I allow myself to experience those feelings, they bring with them a treasure trove of information about how I've been neglecting my own needs or what I'm missing in my life.

Usually, that underlying fear, anger, or uncertainty isn't what is trying to be communicated to me; those feelings open the door for me to look more closely at my own life. This then gives me an opportunity to go find these things. It's not a fast process, which is what makes doing it so hard, but once I allow it to do its thing, the feelings start to subside and transform into newer, lighter feelings.

Throughout this whole process, I can still use the same system to identify my intuition. Even when depressed, I can locate my intuition by looking for the emotionally neutral, calming feeling in the pit of my stomach. Often when I'm depressed, all it shows up to say is, *Don't fear this darkness, it will pass.* That's enough for me in the moment, and because I've learned to establish faith in my inner knowing, I wait, like the voice asks me to, and inevitably it does pass.

For some people, managing anxiety or depression requires the assistance of mental health professionals and medication. This is completely normal, and everyone's situation is different; having professional assistance can be hugely helpful when we're stuck. We need help to unstick ourselves so we can continue to get into the flow of life. But when we are back in flow, I do believe that having a strong connection to your Higher Self and its intuitive guidance helps balance some of these struggles. When balanced with the right treatments and tools for each unique case, our intuition is part of the equation to achieving an optimal state of mental health.

Now that you've created space by addressing your limiting beliefs, your Higher Self will continue to communicate to you with that same levelheaded neutrality. As it does, tune in and start to take action with its guidance. Whenever fear creeps in, you know what to do: repeat the process.

There are three different ways to sense your intuition, but it doesn't mean that you will sense it in all three ways, simultaneously or maybe ever. Your Higher Self and the way it communicates to you through intuition is unique to you. This is why it's so important to learn to trust yourself and be curious about your own process rather than have it prescribed to you by an expert.

You hold the answers and your curiosity about yourself will help you unlock them. The more you come to know yourself, the more easily you will connect to your intuition without doubt or question. That is true empowerment, to know when your inner wisdom is speaking and that you can trust it without anyone giving you permission to do so.

EXPLORATION: *the Spectrum Exercise*

This is the first exercise I teach my clients during our work together. This tool helps to differentiate between the feelings that come with fear versus those that come from our intuition.

Try to find a quiet space to do this exercise so you can really tune in and experience both sides of this spectrum within yourself.

- Take out a piece of paper and draw a line down the middle. On the left write the words *Fear Self*. On the right side of the line write Higher Self.
- Read the rest of these instructions and then do this exercise with your eyes closed.
- Recall a decision that's been weighing on you or something you're looking for clarity on.
- With your eyes closed think of this decision or idea and turn your head to the left. Now say, either out loud or in your head, "Come on, fear, tell me everything you have to say about this."
- Make note of all the thoughts that come in:
  - *As you're having these fear thoughts, stop and make note of your body; where do you feel these ideas affecting your body?*
  - *Now, make note of your energy; how is your energy feeling?*
  - *Last, make note of your emotions; how do you feel emotionally?*
- Open your eyes and make these notes on the left side of your sheet.
- Now, let's repeat the exercise with Higher Self.
- With your eyes closed think of the same decision or idea and turn your head to the right. Now take a very deep breath and say, either out loud or in your head, "Come on, Higher Self, tell me everything you have to say about this."
- Make note of all the thoughts that come in:
  - *As you're having these knowing thoughts, stop and make note of your body; where do you feel these ideas affecting your body?*
  - *Now, make note of your emotions; how do you feel emotionally?*
  - *Last, make note of your energy; how is your energy feeling?*
- Open your eyes and make these notes on the right side of your sheet.

Take some time to examine the difference between the two sides. This is your cheat sheet; this is how you will know to distinguish fear from intuition as you move forward.

CHAPTER 11

# Trust and Faith

On *that very first visit* with Rhea, where she predicted the end of my first marriage, she told me many, many other things. Things about the past and the future that seemed as though someone had sent her a movie of my life before I walked in. She talked to my sister and me about our distant relationship as children. She narrated my parents' divorce and our move across the country as if she'd been there the whole time. She told my sister and me that even though life circumstances sent us in two different directions in our childhood, the rest of our lives was about navigating life together (this couldn't be truer today).

She told me I'd be getting a promotion at work, one that did come three months after that reading, and that sometime after that promotion, I would find the strength to leave my husband. She described what the separation would be like, what behavior I could expect from him and the kids. Sure enough, when the time finally did come, they behaved exactly as she described, almost like she'd handed them a script.

"You know," she said at the end of the reading, "you're meant to teach people how to come back to themselves. One day you'll do that, and many people will know you and your work."

I was working in PR, and that did *not* seem likely. But something in me trusted her, not only because she described my life to me with such accuracy, but because when she looked at me something inside me was set ablaze. In Rhea's presence, my Higher Self sprang to life. With each knowing glance, each prophetic word, Rhea reminded me of what my Higher Self had been whispering all along:

*Come, there's more out there. A lot more.*

How easy is it to write that story off as crazy? Very! I did it myself the moment I left Rhea's house.

*How can any of that be real?* I thought. *She must have some trick.*

I went even lower. *Did Lea talk to her?* I wondered.

Of course, Lea had not called her beforehand. No one was out to scam me. That experience was very real. So was the voice inside gently pulling me toward what was next, toward my evolution and ultimately, my true purpose.

Believing that it was all crazy made it easy to ignore that voice, to not make the decision I knew had to be made. But the voice never quite went away after that. I couldn't ignore it any longer. The more I listened, the louder it got. The more I believed in its existence and trusted that its guidance was in my absolute best interest, the clearer its directions became. Though my Higher Self had been easy to overlook because I didn't want to hear what she wanted me to know, once Rhea had reconnected me to her, I couldn't ignore her, or her guidance, any longer. The first stop on her GPS: real love, the healed kind I told you about before.

When I first met my current husband, TJ, I forgot that Rhea had told me about him three months before. We were sitting on her couch one afternoon two years after that first reading, a year into my divorce, and I was telling her how ready I was for a partner, a true partner in life.

She looked up over my head out the window behind me and said in the calmest voice, as if she were telling me it was raining outside: "He's there. He lives somewhere in Northern California, and he has two boys and he's waiting for you."

Three months later, I found myself standing in the San Francisco office of my agency listening to TJ tell me all about the account I was inheriting from him. He was just so kind, was all I could think. I've told you enough about the competitiveness at my old agency to guess that when people were handing their accounts over to you, they weren't nice about it. But here he was, didn't know a single thing about me, and he had taken the time to pull together a binder full of information to make sure I would succeed.

As he spoke, I looked over at his desk, a tidy desk with three silver frames—one of two little boys.

*Hmmm*, I thought. *San Francisco, two little boys . . . is this . . . ?*

Then I scanned the other pictures; there was a second frame, a photo of TJ skiing with another guy, and then a third of a family—TJ, his wife, and the same two boys from the first picture.

*Definitely NOT*, I thought.

I left his office and San Francisco ready to focus on my new account and didn't really make much of that meeting.

Months passed until I saw TJ again. In those months I continued to see Rhea, get reacquainted with Higher Self, follow her call clearly through hard decisions about my divorce, co-parenting, and my growing career. Life had an entirely new shimmer to it. I felt tuned in, like there was a new hum to my life. Yes, I wanted a partner to experience it all with, but for the first time in my life, I was getting to know me, who I was, without identifying as someone's partner.

Besides, despite being terrified of being a single mom like my own mother had been, I was really enjoying the life Reina, Kian, and I had. We'd spend hours playing board games after work and school, dancing in the kitchen while I made dinner, and adventuring around our neighborhood on warm weeknights in the summer.

Life was good. I was good. That's when healed love is most attracted to us. When our frequency vibrates wholeness.

When my client asked both me and TJ to come to London for a meeting, I thought nothing of it, Rhea's prediction long forgotten. It was there in London, as we worked together, ate meals and entertained clients together, that TJ started to ask me questions about the shimmer.

"How do you seem so good after a recent divorce?"

"Is co-parenting hard?"

"How are the kids handling it, being so young?"

Was he curious about me or was there something else going on that I didn't understand?

London turned to New York, to Barcelona, to Beijing, and before I knew it, I had traveled around the world, falling in love with someone who I was definitely not supposed to be in love with.

It was back in New York when TJ finally told me his feelings for me. He told me that before we met, he'd been trying to work a way out of his marriage, that he just hadn't felt like his real self for too long. As much as I wanted this love, as lonely as I'd felt being a single mom all this time, all I could think of in that moment was my dad, who just hadn't felt right with my mom either.

I opened my mouth to say *absolutely not*, but what came out instead were four words that changed both of our lives.

"You can't have both," I told him.

He knew that. He didn't want to be that person. That's just not who he was.

We said our goodbyes and I felt a little lump form in my throat as I rode the Acela back to DC. It was the first time I'd felt deep love since my marriage, and yet it seemed different, heightened. I didn't know what to do with it. Why would Higher Self lead me to this impossibly heartbreaking situation?

I asked Rhea this later that afternoon, to which she simply replied, "Trust and faith."

It was two weeks later, the end of November, as I sat in my DC office watching the snow fall gently outside the window, when my phone rang. It was TJ. I answered with a tornado of butterflies swirling in the pit of my stomach and there he was on the other side, asking if I had a minute for him.

A minute turned to an hour as I sat and listened to TJ tell me that he had decided to end his marriage, that he had moved out and was calling me from a new apartment. My head was spinning; guilt, shame, excitement, joy, all of it pouring over in nauseating waves inside me.

Higher Self broke in. *Take it slow*, she said. I asked her then, as I sat quietly on that call, to give me the words to respond with and she came through with clarity.

I took a deep breath and told TJ, "If this is real, it needs to be because you are done with your marriage for you, not for me. If that's true, in the six months it takes for your divorce to be finalized, we'll both know it. Call me then, and if you're still in the same place, and you're divorced like me, we can go on a date."

We went on our first date in June.

This isn't a fairy-tale ending by any means. Navigating a new relationship while another was ending was painful for everyone. Reckoning with my own role in the end of a marriage took a lot of honesty and accountability on my part. It also meant not taking on baggage that was not mine, the things that TJ needed to face and own on his healing journey, without me.

There was a lot of separation in the years that followed. TJ and I decided to take it slow, put the kids and each of our healing first, so we navigated a long-distance relationship between California and Maryland for seven years. It needed to be that way. He needed to heal and to do right by his boys, and I needed to make sure nothing ever kept me away from my own expansion ever again. We came to find over those seven years that all we wanted for each other was that expansion, to see the other live in their truth above all else.

Even despite the hardship, the signs were always there that this was a relationship that was in service of our Higher Selves and not counter to them. The biggest one was that our four kids clicked the minute they met, and are still inseparable to this day. Today they are siblings that laugh and fight and make memories together, adding to the quality of one another's lives.

As for me, whenever I had big dreams, TJ was the one who pushed me to go after them, even if it meant leaving him behind at the agency where we both met and starting my coaching practice. For TJ, it was a return to his own Higher Self through this relationship that's changed him. Whenever TJ wants the freedom to spend time alone, and have the chance to finally get to know his Higher Self outside of forced obligations he's put on himself all his life, I've found it easy to just give him that space without fear or need.

We made the choice to navigate whatever life threw at us side by side, with one promise: to always protect each other's relationship with Higher Self, even if it meant getting out of each other's way. Those words were in our vows when we got married nine years later.

Trust and faith, even when they make no f'ing sense. That's the hardest part of the relationships with Higher Self to master once you learn to hear it. Just knowing that you are being guided in accordance to your highest good, at all times, even when it's confusing or painful, is having trust and faith in Higher Self.

My rule with this trust and faith thing is to keep asking at every step, Am I being honest, true to myself and to my values/integrity? If the answer to those things is yes, I keep going, even when the destination is completely out of my sight. I can do this because I have evidence now, in the form of TJ and a relationship I never believed was possible.

This story about TJ is here not as a fairy tale, but as evidence of the trust and faith I'm asking you to give your Higher Self. It's okay if you don't see it unfolding in your life yet; for now, you can borrow my life as your proof.

Belief is everything. My high school history teacher once said, "If you believe it, then it's true." While that maxim is absolutely true when it comes to the limiting beliefs that are implanted in us from the outside, it is just as true when it comes to believing in our own wisdom and ultimately, our Higher Self. *You must believe it exists to even hear it at all.* You have to trust its guidance to truly channel it into making a difference in your life. If you don't believe that it is real, you'll find it easy to ignore.

Similarly, if you don't trust the voice, you'll find it easy to avoid its guidance, to act without checking in with your inner wisdom.

Not trusting the voice is equivalent to not trusting yourself. Believing that somehow your thoughts, desires, and actions are ill-informed, dangerous, or silly is the same thing as not believing that you have any inner wisdom at all. If you truly believed in your Higher Self, in your intuitive wisdom, there's not a shot you would characterize your thoughts, desires, or actions as any of those judgmental things. That's your first test right there. How do you feel about your wants, needs, ideas, and desires? If you're judging them harshly, that's your first sign that you don't quite yet believe in your Higher Self or its language of deeply intuitive and valuable wisdom.

Just a reminder that this lack of faith isn't your fault (at least not completely). Remember that you were trained, by multiple factors in your life, not to trust your inner voice. Now your job is to retrain yourself, to literally rewire your brain to in fact do the opposite of what you were taught. The work now is to learn to believe in the presence of your old, wise friend once again and to trust the guidance that comes from it through your intuitive wisdom.

I won't tell you it's easy. You have decades of training to the contrary, so it will take some work. But just like Rhea did for me, my hope is that this book will allow you to hear the voice of Higher Self in your life again and believe in its existence. Believe that you have something ancient and powerful guiding you, comprised of your own unique energy and essence. Believe that it only wants the best for you, that you are inseparable from it. Believe that the unconditional love it offers is yours for the taking.

It is from that belief that the volume of that intuitive whisper will grow inside you into a resounding voice that is ever-present in your life. That voice will remind you that your truth is the only compass there is, and that your inner peace in living that truth is the only validation you will ever need.

## Using Evidence to Build Trust

Trust and faith—that's what each of our Higher Selves require to communicate with us. However, after years (or decades) of being disconnected from our Higher Selves, it isn't always as easy as just deciding to listen to yourself again. This is a process, and it takes practice. Let's talk practically about how you can begin to cultivate this trust and faith in your own intuitive wisdom.

My favorite way to work my clients through reestablishing trust and faith is by using **evidence**. We've already discussed how evidence is the most powerful tool in retraining ourselves to see our Higher Self as a very real and very valuable part of us. Evidence gives us something tangible to look to in the face of a highly intangible and invisible force that we have been taught to believe is fantasy and make-believe. The good news is that evidence has been piling up over your lifetime, so searching for it shouldn't be too hard.

One afternoon I sat with a client in her home as we searched for this evidence of her Higher Self at work throughout her life. When the session began, she was adamant that there was none. Her life had been hard, she had made "all the wrong decisions," and had been deeply hurt as a result.

"How could my Higher Self, my intuitive wisdom, been present for all those terrible decisions?" she asked me quite cynically.

This is a good question. Why do we make decisions that ultimately create harm or pain for ourselves and for others if our Higher Self is real and present? Shouldn't it have stopped us? How can all those wrong turns and terrible outcomes while Higher Self was along for the ride be possible?

Here's how: because we need to learn to grow, and because those decisions are coming, most often, not from our Higher Self, but from our limiting beliefs—our younger selves. This is why the work on healing those younger aspects who are still trapped in limiting beliefs is so central to the work of connecting to your Higher Self, to your intuitive wisdom. It is critical not only because healing is part of your growth, but because when we don't attend to those younger aspects within, when they are not properly nurtured, they run the show. They will make so much noise that we can't quite hear our Higher Self, and we begin to confuse the voices.

The joy of this work is that people feel comfort in recognizing the love and care Higher Self has shown them in the past. This then generates positive future behavior. If I had this guidance and love even when I wasn't aware of it, what can I do now that I am aware Higher Self is available to me?

Now it's time for you to practice for yourself.

### THE EVIDENCE EXERCISE

It is time to build up your evidence log of just how real your Higher Self really is. Open up that journal, or whatever you've been doing this work in, and free-write your responses to the following prompts:

1. A time when I had a gut feeling or a knowing about something that turned out to be right was . . .
2. A time when I followed my gut feeling or knowing and was pleasantly surprised was . . .
3. A time when I ignored my gut feeling or knowing and was led astray was . . .

Finally, spend a moment and make some promises to yourself. How will you cultivate trust and faith in your own intuitive wisdom? Answer these prompts:

1. I will work on checking in with my own intuition before seeking the opinions of others about decisions I need to make by . . .
2. I will build trust in my intuitive wisdom by following its guidance in this upcoming decision in my life . . .
3. These are the words, or the mantra, I will use when I feel I'm beginning to lose faith in my Higher Self . . .

Some sample mantras for you are:

*I know you're there, I trust you.*

*I am awaiting your guidance.*

*I will trust your guidance.*

*I trust myself and my inner wisdom.*

*I know that the answers are within me.*

### Sustaining Faith in Higher Self

While trust is about believing in your Higher Self and thus your deep intuitive wisdom, faith is about maintaining a sustained belief in its guidance even when things become challenging. Faith is believing that light exists even in the dark. Faith is much harder than trust. Faith requires a deep muscle memory of your intuitive wisdom as having been right when everything in your body wants to go into an instinctual fight-or-flight response. Faith asks that we believe in Higher Self, even when it doesn't make itself abundantly apparent.

The truth is that, even after we learn to believe in our Higher Self and we show that we trust it, there are times where it will feel that it has gone away. That it has abandoned us. It will feel sometimes like the wise whisper has fallen silent when we need it most, when the stakes are highest, and the odds are stacked against us. These are the times we need the loving and powerful guidance of our intuitive wisdom and yet we can't access it. Faith asks us to keep searching, no matter what.

Soon after I met and fell in love with TJ, I started to feel a strong pull away from the East Coast, where I lived and was in the process of raising my young kids. Yes, TJ is from California, but there was more to it than that. TJ lived in the Bay Area when I met him, and it wasn't his California I was feeling pulled toward. Every time I'd think of my ideal life, I would see myself facing the ocean, palm trees swaying in the wind, taking in the sunshine. I would see the kids shining, exploring new parts of themselves, becoming more open and adventurous. The visions played out over and over again for months.

As I began to feel the pull, a strange thing started to happen. Word of mouth about my unique style of coaching began to spread outside the corporate spaces I was so used to operating in. Soon, I found myself sitting across a Zoom call from some very famous faces, the kind of people I was used to seeing on television or the internet.

I had started my career in the entertainment industry, doing marketing for film and television studios, so the presence of entertainers wasn't that strange to me. What was strange is that I never set out to coach them, yet, here I was, building a book of clients in Hollywood and loving every minute of it. Now the pull began to make sense; the West Coast wasn't just what my heart wanted, it was where my career was headed. Heart and head.

Around this same time, I took a trip to Santa Barbara to film a series of courses for LinkedIn Learning. I am not exaggerating when I say that the moment I stepped out of the airport in Santa Barbara I heard that familiar voice: *We belong here.* I was instantly attached to the place. I loved the way it felt, the way it looked, and how I felt being in it.

*Okay,* I thought, *so you love it here and your clients are here, but how in the hell are you going to leave your entire family and move two kids across the country?*

Intuition said it was time, but fear said no way. Fear was filling my head with every single reason this was a terrible idea: *your kids will hate you, your mom will get sick the minute you leave, you'll never make friends like the ones you have here.* So many projections.

The thing is, by this point I had had enough practice listening to my Higher Self and finding evidence that she always led me to a better place that the fear voice was much quieter than my intuitive knowing. The scales had officially flipped; my intuitive wisdom was more powerful than any illusion my fear voice could project.

That didn't mean it was easy. It was one of the hardest things we've been through as a family. That's the thing I want you to know: your Higher Self wants you to achieve your dreams, and it's always working in your favor and in the favor of others, but that doesn't mean your path toward those things will be easy or pretty at all times. This is where trust and faith become your lifeline.

Armed with my intuitive knowing, I finally decided to pull the trigger even though my children's entire lives revolved around the East Coast. As the only biological parent who was responsible for their financial care, I had no choice but to follow where my heart and my career were pulling me. Now imagine telling a thirteen- and an eleven-year-old that they are moving across the country. Not pretty.

My faith in my vision, where my intuition was leading us, wasn't necessarily comforting to them. I could see their lives out west. I sensed deeply how good it would be for them, yet their pain made it hard to believe in my own intuition. Layer on top of that their father, who despite not playing the role of primary caregiver or financial provider, truly and understandably did not want to see them go.

It was a hard road to travel. Lawyers were involved, hurtful words were hurled my way daily, and those two beautiful kids were caught in the cross fire. Every instance they would spend time with Dad, they'd come home, heads full of new fears about moving, each time more terrified than the last. Their fear and their desire to make Dad okay became so overwhelming that they came home one weekend and announced that they had decided to live with Dad. I could go to California on my own.

What had I done? What was I fighting for? This couldn't be the right path.

Higher Self broke through: *Let them be. They are afraid. It will shift.*

Unfortunately, the mom in me, who could not see her life without her children, was louder: *We're not going anywhere! Why are you being so selfish! Just stay put!*

The tension was real. Even with my developed tool kit and years of work around allowing Higher Self to guide, I was struggling. My panic and anxiety threatened to topple me over. Those were dark days. Very dark days. So dark that I, the person who shows people how to reunite with their intuitive wisdom, completely lost sight of my own.

The anxiety was so loud, the exhaustion from being belittled by my ex-husband day in and day out so overwhelming, I just couldn't hear her anymore. It would have been so easy then to believe I had just imagined her all along. That there was no Higher Self guiding me with such precise wisdom. That it was all just a coincidence or, even worse, wishful thinking. Back into another dark night of the soul I went. In those dark days, I doubted my decision to up and move our family, my own career, and even what I was teaching others. I doubted ever listening to her in the first place.

It was also in those dark days that I reached for the people who reminded me of who I was, of how real my Higher Self was and had always been. I reached for Rhea; my cousin, Anais; my sister, Mojgan; my brother, Naheed; my husband, TJ; and my amazing friends. Talking with them always reminded me of the evidence of her existence throughout my life. We listed out that evidence together: how I had trusted her voice when I left a very successful career to coach people; how I listened to her when she told me a more loving, supportive marriage awaited me outside of my first. Every time she told me to take the plunge, it worked out better than my greatest expectations.

In those dark moments, it isn't up to you alone to sustain the faith. Finding reflections of your Higher Self in the people who love you is a necessary and wonderful step. Thanks to their reminders (that her guidance had always been with me and always been right), I pulled myself up and out of that dark, heavy place of doubt and began to look for her again. I looked for her in my moments of silence and in my walks outside among the trees. I looked for her in my children's smiles and even their tears. I looked for her in the songs that came on the radio and the verses that would fall into my lap from spiritual teachers like Rumi, Pema Chödrön, Ekhart Tolle, and Elizabeth Lesser.

I looked for her everywhere. I looked and, in my mind, I'd repeat, "I believe in you, I know you're there." I kept the faith, I kept looking. Sometimes I'd hear nothing but experience a deep peace in return. That's when I knew she was near. Slowly that gave way to hearing her voice over that of my fear again:

*Not only are you going to be okay, you already are okay. You are on your way to being better than okay, and believe me, so are those kids.*

She was right. Now, we are all better than okay.

Living in Santa Barbara has been like transplanting all of us into a garden full of fertilizer. I see each of us blossoming into something new while we find our way in our new surroundings. Reina has made friends, rediscovered her love of music, and is emerging as this confident, witty, self-possessed young woman. Kian is finding his people too and has a peace and joy about him that makes him a constant source of laughter in our house. There's an ease in his spirit that has full permission to expand here.

More than anything, while being away from my family is hard, there's an independence this move has given us to figure out who we are outside of it all. Like we're using the space this distance has created to become even more of that true self. We can always go back home, and we do often, but when we do, it feels like we go back home more whole.

They are, as I had seen in my vision, flourishing, and I get to flourish right alongside them. While my fear voice was saying I had to choose between their happiness or my own, my Higher Self was telling me, all along, that both were possible. My faith in her and the reminders of my loved ones are the only reason I could hear her over the cries of the fear within.

When you face challenges that are particularly triggering, reminding you of the insecurity of your childhood in any way, remember that your childhood self will jump in and begin directing things through limiting beliefs that show up as fear and anxiety. Those are well-practiced voices in your life, voices you have learned to listen to above all else. This will make your Higher Self even harder to hear, and therefore, harder to believe in.

This is when you have to hold on to trust and faith like a lifeline. Trust, as I did and continue to do, the pull of your desires; they are coming from your Higher Self. Trust yourself, above all else and at all times. It's the only way through.

But you're not alone in these dark times; your Higher Self is never far. It is a part of you. It is always communicating to you through intuition. It is your compass at all times, even when you can't hear it. Knowing that the guidance is there but is being blocked out by all your fear will help you remember to acknowledge it. Start there in those times. Even if you can't hear it, know that it can hear you. Speak to it, ask for what you need, ask it to show up in your life. Then, give it room.

Don't give up on your old wise friend again; remember that your belief in it, your faith in it, is all it needs to power through the cacophony of your fear and anxiety voices. Feed it with your faith and watch it guide you endlessly.

EXPLORATION: *Following the Call*

Empowered with your new tools of evidence and faith, it is time to draw yourself a road map to your dreams. This is your time to take all the *can'ts* and *shouldn'ts* and put them aside for a moment. Take some time and a deep breath and do some free-writing answering these prompts:

1. What would I do this year if I knew it would end up a success?
2. Why does doing this matter? How does it make me feel more whole?
3. Who do I imagine I will be after I take this step and it works out? How will I feel?

Now take a big breath and invite Higher Self into the dialogue. Simply ask if your intuitive knowing has anything to add. What does your Higher Self think about this thing you want? Write down everything you get in response.

CHAPTER 12

# Embodying Your Higher Self

Hearing your *Higher Self through* your intuition is the opening to a total life transformation.

This relationship will help you find the scared parts inside and take care of them. It will show you all the projected, limiting beliefs that are keeping you small and guide you to finally letting them go. And ultimately, it will bring you fully into your power and put you squarely on the path toward living your purpose in the most dignified, fulfilled, and authentic way possible.

Being aligned to your Higher Self means being at peace with your truth and empowered to speak that truth openly with confidence and without seeking validation in response. This is why the work of reconnecting to this inner wisdom is so critical and so life-changing.

This is what hundreds of people have accomplished by using my method. This is not just theory—it is now yours to use and to fit to your own needs. In this chapter, we will learn together how to apply this methodology to how you move in your everyday life. From decision-making to acting without attachment, that connection with Higher Self should not only be your source of purpose but also the guiding force in your day-to-day decisions and actions.

## Returning to Your Truth Each Time

Deep down, we all just want to live in our truth. Pretending hurts and is exhausting. Speaking your truth, while scary at first, is a release. Speaking your truth is freedom. Your Higher Self is always completely in line with your truth: who you are deep down, what you truly believe, and what you honestly desire. That is why listening to its language of intuition is such a part of being in your truth. Your Higher Self exists to remind you of that truth and push you toward the decisions that allow it to become fully embodied.

As you learn to work with your limiting beliefs, and thus your fears, you remove their frantic noise from your mind. You get to clearly hear what is true for you. That truth, when it is spoken out loud, is the key to your freedom and your peace of mind. This is how you begin to move from a contracted state of seeking external validation to an open and centered state of embodying your Higher Self: a wise, rooted energy that knows what they want and goes about getting it in a loving and decisive way.

Moving in the world in this way opens your path to your purpose. It is only possible to clearly understand and live your purpose when you are aligned with your truth, when you are acting out of a place of authenticity rather than from a need for others to accept you. It is all connected. Everything I have told you until this point, all of that work, is connected to ultimately hearing and being in your purpose.

Let's put it all together now:

Part One: Identifying Your Fear Self

- Uncovering your limiting beliefs allows you to heal the younger parts of you that are still trapped in painful memories.

Part Two: Healing Your Limiting Beliefs to Create Space for Your Higher Self

- As those aspects are healed, they will make less internal noise and will project less fear and anxiety into your life and your decisions.
- With the space that is created by the decrease in noise from your limiting beliefs, you create a pathway for your Higher Self to speak to you through your intuition about your truth—who you are deep down, what you truly believe, and what you honestly desire.

Part Three: Reconnecting with and Embodying Your Higher Self

- As you begin to embody your Higher Self, standing tall in your truth, your intuitive wisdom can guide you clearly toward your purpose, your reason for existing.
- Living your purpose will create the fulfillment you have been in search of and will create a positive impact on the world around you.

### Intuitive Decision-Making

The embodiment of Higher Self in practical terms means making decisions from your intuitive wisdom with as little doubt or fear as possible—optimally, with no fear or doubt. This can only be done when you acknowledge every aspect of your being, all at once: the fearful, limited versions of your youth and your Higher Self. By doing this, you see that there is more than just one voice guiding your decision. You allow the fear voice to calm down so you can hear all voices.

Working with all your aspects in making a decision means consulting your **inner roundtable.** Think of your inner roundtable as your life's board of directors. Each aspect of you, from your youngest self to your most fearful self to the most empowered, Higher Self, all meet to discuss and debate each and every decision you make. They each have their own needs and interests, and they are all there to ensure at first your survival and, as you heal and become aware of your Higher Self, your ability to thrive.

### THE INNER ROUNDTABLE EXERCISE

Take a pause to picture your inner roundtable now. Start with the furniture. Imagine a round table with chairs plotted neatly along in a circle. Starting from your left, begin to envision each of the younger versions of yourself that you have identified as being still stuck in limiting beliefs. Allow each of them to take a seat at the table.

As you go around the roundtable, see each aspect of you as it grows older and embodies new beliefs. As these aspects grow older, they also begin to hold values that make you truly who you are. As you continue to move around the table, begin to envision these versions of you imbued with these qualities. They can be aspects like your creative side, your intellectual side, your adventurous side, your leader side. These are the aspects that you would use to describe yourself without judgment. Allow them to take the form of you at whatever age you feel you really embodied these qualities and let them also be present at this roundtable.

Finally, in the position where you are currently sitting, envision your Higher Self. However that vision manifests, let it be. Don't question it for now.

Now that everyone is present, we get to work with them all to think through a decision or area in your life where you feel stuck.

Bring that decision or topic to mind. As you move around the roundtable, take a minute to hear what each aspect has to say about it. The aspects on the left side, the younger ones still in limiting beliefs, will likely share their fears about that decision. They will likely list all the ways you could get hurt or all the ways you are not capable or worthy of making this thing happen. Remember, you know now how to listen to those aspects *without* judgment.

As you listen, ask them what they *really* need beneath the fear. They may say things like *to have more fun in life, to slow down, to be connected to others.* These will be very basic needs that they would use the language of a child to ask for. Register their needs and continue to move around the table.

As you approach the aspects of you that embody the qualities that make you who you are, that represent your values in life, check in with what each of these aspects thinks and needs in the situation. I'll use myself as an example to help make this more tangible. The greatest thing I value in life is freedom: freedom to say, do, and be what I want. To go where I please. To work in a way that's most fulfilling to me.

Most important, I value freedom when it comes to my time. I need the freedom of time to wander and be spontaneous, to feel like my life is full of surprises and experiences that make me feel connected to the world around me. Basically, I need freedom to feel truly fulfilled, so much so, the word *freedom*—in Farsi, *azadi*—is tattooed on my wrist.

I see this aspect of me as being most alive at the age of seventeen. That is when I embodied this value with such force that I resembled a wild horse galloping toward whatever called to me with such a fury, everyone had to get out of my way. So, in my roundtable exercise, when I am checking in with this important value of freedom, I stop to hear what a seventeen-year-old version of me would want me to consider so that my need for freedom is also being considered in the decision.

As you move along your roundtable and hear each version out, you will land on your Higher Self. Take your deep, cleansing breath and register the very first emotionally neutral thought that comes to you about the decision.

Now that you have heard out every version of you, you have all the information you need to make an intuitively informed decision. You have heard the needs of your younger selves and your values, or archetypes, and you have heard what your Higher Self has to say through your intuition. Can you make the decision that needs to be made in the way your Higher Self has told you to, while getting the needs of all your aspects met? Absolutely! This is where the roundtable can begin to negotiate.

Maybe some elements of the decision need to be done in a certain way or with certain timing to make sure your needs are met. Maybe you'll feel that all aspects are ready to move forward now that they've heard the wise and calming voice of Higher Self. Either way, you have just bypassed the paralysis and anxiety that come from only listening to your limited selves in fragments or on loop.

Now that all aspects of you are present at the roundtable, no one limited aspect can take over, shouting and creating so much noise that you can't hear your intuitive wisdom. Since you've heard them all out, not only can you make an intuitive decision from a place of calm and knowing, you can also meet the needs of all your inner aspects. It's a win-win.

### Action Without Attachment: Losing the When and How

The process of taking intuitive action and being met with opportunity beyond our wildest dreams really is that accessible. It comes down to working with fear while listening to—and following—Higher Self with trust and faith. It is a dual process at all times. As you work through the process, however, it becomes faster and more organic. Eventually, it evolves into an innate part of your thought process that doesn't require much of your focus.

Great! It must feel gratifying and like magic all the time, right?

Not exactly.

While connecting with and following the guidance of our Higher Self truly is an act of connecting to our own divinity, we are all still human. As humans we have been trained to only believe in what we can see, which means we require immediate evidence that our intuitive decisions are manifesting in the life of our dreams. Instant gratification. Some need it more than others. I am hugely guilty of getting caught on this part.

When I first left the agency and started my own consulting firm, I could feel intuitively that I was meant to help people come back to their own inner wisdom and create real impact from a place of purpose. I knew that soon I'd meet magnificent, impressive clients who inspired the world. I felt so strongly that was who I was meant to coach, and that I could use my intuitive gifts to teach them how to find and use their own. I couldn't have left my job had I not felt that secure in my intuition.

So, I left to be an intuitive purpose coach! And then... I waited. I had a good method, good contacts from my decades of agency work, and yet, no one understood my message. Intuitive leadership sounded like a new woke trend for people to laugh off, roll their eyes at, and ignore. I couldn't just wait around. I needed to make money. I was supporting myself and two kids. My Higher Self had said it would come. *What the f#@k?!* I thought. I had left my job, I had my Higher Self's guidance pushing me clearly in this direction, and yet, not many clients were coming. There were some, but the work I did with them felt enough like the work from my previous, agency job that I began to worry.

Well, not the clients I imagined came, anyway. Instead, founders of small- to medium-size businesses found me. They needed help managing change and crisis inside their companies, they needed help building morale with their employees, and they were ready and willing to pay. It was the opportunity that was available to me, so I took it. I spent the first three years only doing this kind of work, creating strategies and message points, training CEOs on speeches and hard conversations with staff, even overhauling one organization's entire marketing team. It paid well, but it also felt like exactly what I was doing at the agency I had just left, just with way more stress about paying the bills.

I started to wonder if I'd ever achieve that intuitive vision I had, the one that jolted me up and out of a safe career with the promise of something radical. A chance to own my gifts out loud and help others do the same. It was starting to feel like a mirage, and like I was a fool for upending my whole career to pursue it. That's the thing with listening to your Higher Self; there's no assurance that there will be an immediate payoff. You just have to keep listening, following every little sign you get, and work your darndest to be patient.

I am not good at being patient. This is where it started to feel murky for me—and where it does for many of my clients. My anxiety told me constantly that I'd been naive, that I should think more clearly, that I'd never "make it" the way I envisioned. It's not easy when anxiety is beating you down like this. It's terrifying when the fears of financial ruin haunt you like monsters emerging from under your bed while you lay awake at night.

All of this was happening *while* I continued to listen to my Higher Self. It felt like living two lives. I'd wake up centered and assured by her guidance and end the day wanting to curl up in the fetal position, exhausted from believing all the fear and anxiety projections. It is so challenging to feel confident in yourself—and your path forward—when your limiting beliefs crop up to tell you that you're wrong. But, if you keep trusting your own inner wisdom, following your Higher Self pays off. Maybe you don't get the thing you wanted right away, but you're empowered to leave a job that is no longer serving you. Maybe you don't get the thing you wanted *at all*, and you find something that fits you even better.

Of course, I didn't have that perspective when I was just feeling impatient.

In the midst of this inner battle, I experienced a game-changing moment: I met Alok Vaid-Menon.

We were at an event hosted by one of my clients, and I noticed Alok immediately when I first saw their bright dress and pink hair. They walked into the auditorium, and I watched as they smiled at people who were excited to meet them, posed for photos, and took their seat in the front row preparing for their upcoming talk on the main stage. What I was not prepared for was the experience of hearing Alok speak. Alok, a performer, poet, and activist, was known around the world for their powerful way with words, and the way they used those words to reach into your heart and force you to face your truth.

As I sat and listened to Alok recite a powerful poem about the transformative power of grief, I felt the voice inside again—*Pay attention*, said Higher Self. That was it. Just: *Pay attention to this person.*

The event continued with powerful speaker after powerful speaker, after which we were dismissed to our rooms to get ready for the final event, the gala. I entered the gala slightly intimidated by my fashion choice among this glitzy crowd. I stood in the middle of the room, sipping my tequila and lime, chatting with my clients when I felt this force move toward me with a rush of energy. The next thing I knew, Alok was standing next to me.

"Hi!" they said brightly "I've been wanting to talk to you!"

"Me?" I asked, sure that Alok had mistaken me for someone of actual notoriety in this group of impressive people.

"Yes!" they continued. "I'm so intrigued by what you do! Crisis management. Fascinating."

"Erm, yeah, I guess," I mumbled.

"I'd love to keep talking; shall we trade info?" they asked.

*DUH! YES!* I wanted to scream, but instead managed to somehow keep my cool and give Alok my email, fully expecting to never hear from them again. I was so taken aback by their curiosity and their openness that the rest of the night was a blur.

I came home two days later full of inspiration from all that I had learned. That was enough to gain from the trip, I thought. But, to my surprise, within a week, there in my inbox was an email from Alok asking if we could schedule a call. When we finally met, we learned we had a lot in common, from our cultural upbringing to our views of the world. I started to offer Alok advice about their career as a highly visible and unfairly targeted nonbinary artist and performer.

I kept things corporate, offering messaging and media advice. The past three years had taught me that no one was interested in my intuitive gifts or the more spiritual side of what I could really do. But, as we'd talk, Alok would push me.

"There's more to you," they'd say, "I just know it."

How long could I play dumb? One day I blurted out, "I'm intuitive and really my dream is to teach leaders and others how to find and follow their intuition."

"Okay!" Alok said, beaming. "NOW WE ARE TALKING!"

I will never forget that moment where Alok really saw me. They saw my gift so clearly that of course they believed me when I shared my dream.

I started really coaching Alok then, in the method I wanted, in the method I've since used to coach hundreds of people. I watched them transform in front of my eyes, the story of which is not mine to tell, but theirs. From this transformation, Alok became determined to let the world know who I was and what gift I had to offer them.

We joke now that Alok is my agent. They've sent me some of the most challenging and spiritually gifted clients I have had the pleasure of coaching. That dream my Higher Self had whispered to me when I was quitting my job all those years ago was coming to fruition, and it happened neither when nor how I had imagined.

That's the thing about following your intuition: you have to do it with trust and faith while completely detaching from the *when* and the *how*. Those things are not for you to worry about. Your job is to get very clear on the *what* and let go of the rest. When you let your truth inform you about *what* you want, when you listen to your desires and keep faith in your intuitive wisdom, the *when* and the *how* always work themselves out.

You just have to keep moving with your inner wisdom as your guide, following it in every step. My Higher Self told me to pay attention to Alok, so when Alok began to guide me, I listened. I couldn't have guessed that they were my *how*. If my Higher Self had told me that level of specificity three years prior, I may not have resonated with it because I expected the process to come about differently and could have resisted the information. That's the first reason not to worry about the *when* and the *how*. You may not be ready for the full picture at that moment; you may only be ready for the very next step.

Which takes me to the second reason why the *when* and *how* are not yours to worry about: you still have lessons to learn to prepare you for the things you want. Your Higher Self is most interested in moving you toward your desires, but it knows that the only way to do that is by walking you through the labyrinth that holds each lesson you need to learn to receive the things you want. As you twist and turn through the maze, you have new experiences. You're challenged and, in those challenges, you begin to learn more about who you really are and what you're capable of. These are lessons that are priceless to your growth.

Remember your soul wants you to grow and expand, which makes these lessons, as difficult as they may be, a critical part of your spiritual process. As you learn these lessons, you become better prepared, full of new information about your grit, your resilience, the depth of your desires, and so much more. This newly found awareness is what prepares you for the dream when it finally arrives. Those lessons are what prepare you for the opportunities that come your way and allow you to use them to catapult toward the life you desire.

I know it sounds counterintuitive but trust me: there is nothing worse than getting what you want when you're not ready. When that happens, you can't make the most of that opportunity. It doesn't become as fruitful or fulfilling as it could. Your Higher Self doesn't want that for you. It doesn't want to see you squander opportunities that lead to your self-realization, so it guides you through the path that is full of these gems: the life lessons. Everything is happening in its right time and in ways that you can't even conceive of until you're ready to understand them.

Knowing this will let you follow your Higher Self, that powerful intuitive wisdom, while detaching from the process. This is such a critical part of getting to where you want. Once you learn to let go of the stronghold you have on the process, you free things up to move toward you more easily. You remove the energetic obstacles you've unknowingly put in place. Best yet, you get to live in the moment. Worrying about *when* and *how* is such a thief of joy. That constant worrying is what is robbing you of your ability to live your life in this very moment.

That is all there is: the here and now. When you learn to hear and follow your intuition with complete trust and faith and let go of the *when* and *how*, you free up space to experience your life as it is happening. When the worries subside, you have more room to notice the tiny details of life—which is where the joy lies.

And, you know what? The life you're living today, the one that feels like a stop along a path to your dreams, this life right now is one your past self dreamt of. Would your past self want to just enjoy this life instead of worrying about what's next? I bet the answer is yes.

Know this: practicing this presence now all but ensures that you will enjoy your dreams as they become manifest too. You are training yourself now to be in the moment, and as you enjoy your life, your dreams move closer, and when they arrive, you have already practiced how to experience and enjoy them fully.

### Ritualizing Your Connection

As you begin to reunite with Higher Self, you might find yourself feeling especially energized. The exuberance can be almost childlike as you remember the joy inherent to expansion, and of feeling like possibilities are limitless. As you experience this reconnection with yourself, you become certain that you can never go back to being separated from your Higher Self.

But there will be moments that test you.

That's because we all live here on Earth, a planet full of others who have not awoken to that reality and who will continue to project limiting beliefs, scarcity, and doubt onto us. In addition, we have complicated lives, responsibilities to maintain, bills to pay, and people to care for. All of these things require so much of our energy that it can be incredibly challenging to remain connected to Higher Self at all times.

That's okay. More important, it's normal. Promise me you won't be hard on yourself when this happens to you. It still happens to me. Remember that it is easy for this to happen because you have been trained to put others' needs and opinions before your own.

This is your training. While you now have awareness about how to heal those limiting beliefs, you will get triggered back into believing them from time to time. You will be exhausted or sad or anxious, and, in those moments, you will forget to check in with Higher Self. No stress. Higher Self is still there, still sharing its loving guidance, and when you create space it will break through just like before.

I ask my clients to create this space by ritualizing their connection to their Higher Self. This doesn't have to be some elaborate ritual that involves incense and crystals. Don't get me wrong—I love a good meditation with incense and crystals (just ask the humans and animals that live with me), but it's not necessary nor will it work if it is not authentic to who you are. Your ritual is exactly that—yours. It can be short and sweet or as long and spacious as you need. Whichever way you do it, it just needs to have three common elements:

1. **A QUIET SPACE**—It's important that you find a break from the noise, internal and external, to make room for your Higher Self and you to connect. This can be a morning meditation, sitting outside with a coffee, a walk after dinner, or taking ten minutes to get up from your desk and walk around the room away from others. Whatever it is, your goal is to ensure you have a quiet space to hear your Higher Self and really let its guidance sink in.

2. **DEEP BREATHS**—Breathing is not something we often have to think about. In fact, thinking about it can even make it feel harder to do. But just like we don't think about the act of breathing, we also don't think about the quality of our breaths. Most of our breaths are short and shallow, just the right amount to get us the oxygen we need but not enough to slow our heart rate or our racing thoughts. Breathing can be a powerful way to create inner peace and make room for Higher Self when it is done with intention. Here is the simple breathing exercise I do with my clients before I ask them to check in with Higher Self:

    1. *Close your eyes and very slowly breathe through your nose, envisioning your chest growing and expanding with air.*

II. *Keep breathing in slowly until you feel your chest is fully expanded.*

III. *Hold your breath for two full seconds.*

IV. *Blow the air out of your mouth fully and powerfully.*

V. *Repeat two more times.*

This exercise does wonders to clear the noise in your mind, so please use it all day long or as much as you need.

The other thing about this breathing exercise is that when you do it right before checking in with Higher Self, it starts to become a signal to your brain that this breathwork is synonymous with aligning with your inner wisdom, your intuitive thoughts. Your brain will perceive these three deep breaths as a notification: *It's time! Let's listen for intuition now.*

3. **A SIGN OF RECOGNITION**—As you clear your mind you can ask your Higher Self in any way you're most comfortable with to come through. This can be by asking it a question or simply by saying something like: "I'm here to listen." That is your opener. As you receive the intuitive thoughts or feelings, you need a signal to yourself that you're really taking them in. I, for example, will nod. Others will put their hands on their heart or together in gratitude. Some might say something out loud like "Got it" or "Thank you." Whatever feels most natural to you, find a way to show recognition of the intuitive thought in the moment. This will seal the thought into your mind, allowing you to recall the information when you need it most.

The fluidity of this ritual exercise is purposeful because there is no ritual that can be prescribed for you about how to access your own intuition. After all, we are impacted by different people, systems, and situations every day; the ways in which we will be triggered can shift from day to day. Really, this ritual is about finding opportunities to be connected to your Higher Self—feeling comfortable and authentic—*despite* all the noise around you.

For example, this is why I don't force my clients to meditate. While meditation is an incredible tool I myself use to still my mind and connect to my Higher Self, it doesn't always work for everyone. What's more important is that you find the right ritual. That's the whole point of connecting to your Higher Self: to look for the answers from within instead of being told how to do it from the outside. Think about what makes you feel calm and centered. If it is meditation, great! If it's going on a run, great! Listening to a record? Also great. Whatever connects you, that is the right way. No one has the answer but you.

Regardless of how you do it, the goal is to make sure you are creating space for your Higher Self in your busy and complicated life. While it might be hard to do at first, once you create that time and space consistently to sit with Higher Self, you will notice a difference in the way you feel and how accessible the feeling of calm is to you. You will notice how many answers you truly have inside you and begin to seek them from others less.

Most important, you will begin to feel empowered about the hard decisions you have to make, seeing that through this consistent connection you are more able to make clear, intuitive decisions that feel good. You will have faith in your decisions as you watch them turn into incredible outcomes. That is the importance of making connecting to your Higher Self a daily practice: the whole is greater than the sum of its parts.

CHAPTER 13

# Changing Frequencies Means Changing Relationships

**W**e, *each and every one* of us, deserves to experience our lives in the fullness of all they have to offer, without limitation.

But like we just talked about, staying in this connection while navigating the outside world is profoundly tricky. Not just because of the average stresses of our lives either, but because we are relational beings, and we live in relationship to other humans. We are interdependent. Your awakening to your Higher Self does not assure the same awakening to those you are in relationship with. Which means you have to get comfortable expanding to this version of yourself, even if those around you are not there yet.

Not everyone will have access to their Higher Self like you. Some may not even have the awareness that they have a Higher Self, but may still be trapped in the projections of their limiting beliefs. You don't have to let these people go from your life. You just have to learn how to keep them from blocking your growth while having the compassion and trust that their journey will bring them to their Higher Self, just as yours did for you.

The path may be rocky, and some relationships will be challenged, but those challenges are necessary. Your expansion into your Higher Self will do one of two things: clear the people from your life who cannot honor your truth or inspire them to discover and live by their own and grow alongside you.

As you come back into alignment with your Higher Self, a shift will become evident to the people around you. This shift can be subtle or dramatic. For example, once I stepped into alignment with my Higher Self I began to have harder boundaries around my time, and I'd let people know if they were asking too much of me. I'd say no much more frequently.

People noticed. Sometimes they'd let me know that they were hurt or that I felt less available to them; they weren't used to me choosing my own needs over theirs. That wasn't always comfortable for me to hear, nor did I always know how to navigate it.

If I'm being really honest with myself, I still get caught up here when I think something I am doing for my highest good will make someone else uncomfortable. I spend an inordinate amount of time fretting about it. This doesn't stop me from doing the thing, but the way people react to me still affects me, even as I step into Higher Self more fully.

That's what's most important to remember at this part of the path: you can't foretell how people will react, but sometimes the fear of their reactions can be a stumbling block on this path to living as your Higher Self.

I notice in my own life and in my clients' lives that this fear of others' reactions to our expansion can really limit how often we allow ourselves to embody Higher Self. Even after all the work we do to heal our limiting beliefs and make intuitive decisions guided by this inner wisdom, we can easily revert back to our more limited frequencies out of a desire to please others and keep them comfortable.

That is totally understandable. We want to belong and a lot of us have little people pleasers inside who tell us that other people's comfort matters much more than living our truth. But here's the thing: growth, in every instance, requires some discomfort. When any organism is growing, that process is uncomfortable. A snake shedding its skin is probably not enjoying losing an outer layer that's been attached to its body. A caterpillar stuck in a cocoon may feel tightly bound in that space. As your own body grew as a kid, it hurt; that's why they call it growing pains.

Growth is discomfort. So, when we want others to remain comfortable, what we are actually saying to them, beneath our efforts to keep them comfortable with us, is that we don't want *them* to grow as humans. How often do you consider other people's comfort when you're making a decision or communicating your thoughts? That's it, right there, that holding back of your truth to keep people comfortable. That's you saying to them: "I don't want you to grow. Stay small, it's all I think you're capable of."

### Your Truth Will Set Them Free Too

I learned how to tell the truth from my sister. As we got older and closer, my sister modeled something unheard-of for me: living your truth mattered more than people accepting you. This wasn't an easy lesson for her, or us as a family. She came to this realization in her own journey, a story that I think she should tell, but I can say this much: coming out as queer in your thirties when you're married with a one-year-old son is close to impossible, and yet my sister did it.

We didn't make it easy for her, my mom and I. We couldn't understand how, in our minds, she had been one thing for twenty-nine years and then could just become another. This, of course, was my nineteen-year-old brain at work, not understanding the coming-out process as I do now, having no awareness of the heaviness people carry all their lives as they battle with their own truth and the need for other people's acceptance and love. At that time in my life, I felt like my sister was being selfish, if I'm honest. I worried about my nephew, felt heartbroken for my brother-in-law, and thought that my sister should just "suck it up" and conform to the family life society had laid out for her.

I tell this story now from a completely different vantage point, trying hard not to judge that nineteen-year-old with these hurtful limiting beliefs. It's hard to admit that, once upon a time, I had been so deeply indoctrinated that I, of all people, was the voice of bondage and conformity I'm working so hard to free clients from today. Sadly, for my sister, my mom and I chose fear over love. We took our love away. We stopped speaking to her for months. We tended to the broken heart of my brother-in-law and the growing heart inside my tiny nephew instead. We left my sister to tend to her own brokenness alone.

It crushes me every time I think that we did that to her, but my sister marched on. She kept her eye on her truth. She fought for it, and she showed us while she did that, that she could love us and be in her truth at the same time. That her coming-out didn't mean the person we knew was lost to us. That in fact, living in her truth made her more herself, more available to us as a whole person, not just the fraction of her we had mistaken for her full self.

It took time, and a lot of love and patience on her side. Ultimately, it took a lot of love from us too, but we got there. We understood her, we saw the error of our ways, and we expanded our view. We expanded our whole selves to make room for this new reality—but only because my sister refused to budge from her truth.

That was uncomfortable. Not just telling you that story, but the entire process of living that story. It was heart-wrenching and awkward. It was so damn uncomfortable that four entire people expanded into a whole new frequency because of it. My sister, standing in her truth, demanded that we raise ourselves up, past our fear and our need for comfort, into our own highest frequency.

It took me time and my own dark night of the soul through my divorce to realize that through her insistence that she be allowed to be loved for who she was, my sister was showing me that I too deserved that right, that everyone deserved it. Her determination to make us look at our own fears caused me to go searching for my Higher Self. Yes, because I didn't want to lose my sister, but also because she was showing me how free I could be. What if she had backed down, backed into a life that kept her hidden, living a lie? Who would I be today if she hadn't shown me the path to my Higher Self just by holding strong to her own truth, even as those she loved couldn't quite understand or love her for it?

Her truth set me free, and your truth, whatever it is, will do that for the people you love, the ones who really love you. That's a hard possibility to believe. It's hard to have faith that being yourself won't make people go away. That's what you've been trained to believe: that love is scarce, and your truth won't cut it. As you read these words, I am willing to bet that you can literally feel the spectrum we've talked about pulling inside you. On one side there is your Higher Self, excited that you are being encouraged to really examine what living fully in your truth would look like. On the other side are all those sweet little selves, full of limiting beliefs, desperate for love and acceptance, starting to get a little nervous again.

Just a reminder that it's okay that our little selves are activated. They need to come along for this ride too, and they have needs that require our attention. Here's a reminder for those little selves: you can have it all. Their needs can be met, and you can thrive. They just have to let go and let your Higher Self drive.

### Your People Pleaser Won't Like This

Embodying your Higher Self, which is the same as living your truth unabashedly, is in many ways about being a leader. You are here to awaken others to their own limitlessness by embracing your own. That can't happen without leadership. Being a leader in your life means finding your truth and embodying it so that others can watch you and understand that it's possible. It means you don't slow down to make sure everyone around you is comfortable with who you are and how you live.

When you are in alignment with Higher Self, you are making decisions from your own inner wisdom instead of conforming to what others say. I won't lie to you: when you do that, it will undoubtedly make people uncomfortable. Here's the good news: their discomfort has absolutely nothing to do with you.

That discomfort is simply about others not being awakened, yet, to their own Higher Self, and therefore not understanding how you can be forging your own path in a way that may seem to them brazen, lacking the shame they feel we all should have when we live our truth out loud. When people don't understand, it makes them uncomfortable, and when they're uncomfortable, they will judge as a means to protect themselves from the fear you're bringing up in them.

Remember, judgment is an internal projection directed outward. It is only possible to judge others harshly because you are judging yourself harshly. This reminder is meant to help you put other people's judgments of you into context; they are reflecting their own limiting beliefs and shame onto you. It's not about you. It's never about you.

Knowing that's where their judgment comes from, can you see how harmful a message it is, to send in response to people's judgment, that you will shrink and hide your Higher Self? That tells them that they should be full of shame about their own Higher Self, their own truth. When instead we model what it looks like to stand firmly in our inner wisdom and our truth, we show others that it is okay to do the same, that they shouldn't judge their own truth so harshly.

Now, let me warn you, your internal people pleaser won't like this. It's probably in there right now, screaming at you to put this book down. Maybe its convincing you that I don't know what I'm talking about, or that it is easy for me to say because I don't know your life or what's at stake. That's fine. Your people pleaser is just doing its job.

*Good job, little one, you're trying to protect like you think you should.*

The amazing performer and content creator Dylan Mulvaney is one of my favorite clients and friends. She's done the hard work to overcome this very thing. Dylan is a trans woman who detailed her transition in her TikTok series, "365 Days of Girlhood." Her honest, vulnerable, and hilarious videos won people over quickly, and I mean quickly. Throughout that year, thanks to living her truth so publicly, Dylan got over 13 million followers. Her life transformed practically overnight, which didn't give her, or anyone, enough time for the inner world to catch up to the outer one.

When she came to me, the little people pleaser inside was in overdrive. This younger aspect who was so desperate to be seen and loved for who she was wanted Dylan to keep cranking out the content that got her the likes, without a break, without rest. Yet, Dylan was feeling pulled toward more. A trained theater performer and incredible actress and singer, Dylan was being pushed by her Higher Self to explore new avenues to connect with her audience while pursuing her greatest dreams. This meant being even more publicly open and honest about her truth.

Sadly, we live in a society that doesn't always meet this level of truth with open arms. Dylan receives death threats almost daily from people who so deeply fear their own truth they've decided it is easier to take that fear, alchemize it into hatred, and hurl it at a beautiful, kind, gentle, and incredibly talented soul who is here to help us all access our own joy and our own truth. This is what she lives with, and yet, through our work together, she digs in, finds that people pleaser who is often terrified at the reactions she gets, and lovingly coaxes her out.

In this work, Dylan beautifully demonstrates how, by identifying that her people pleaser is an aspect of her younger self just playing out a survival strategy, she can give that aspect the love and understanding she's been waiting for. When she does that, her ability to listen and embody her Higher Self expands tenfold, even though she is keenly aware it makes some people uncomfortable. This is the resilience we can experience when we do this work, and it is through this resilience that people like Dylan show us the path to our own freedom.

## *Boundaries, Baby*

Let's get practical about how you can do this because I know it's hard. To embody your Higher Self without too much regard for others' reactions, you have to create space. This space is your arena to explore who you are, try and fail, speak up, pursue your dreams, and ultimately, grow more fully into yourself. Arenas have boundaries, walls that separate the outer world from whatever happens inside that space. So, you too must construct and uphold boundaries. Boundaries don't have to be difficult. You can start slow and continue to build them as you go.

As you think about the boundaries you need to give yourself room, I want to offer you three ways to think about constructing your boundaries.

### NEEDS

Your needs are the foundation for your boundaries. Duh, right? Well, not so much. We don't really stop to assess our own needs as much as you would think. We are in such constant reaction mode to the world around us that what we actually need in a given moment is predominately lost to us, so we find it difficult to create boundaries.

I've told you in this book exactly why you do this (all the conditioning that's required you to give up your needs), so I won't repeat that again. What matters now is that, being aware of that conditioning, you begin to reject those outside implants so you can tune in to what you really need in your life.

Think about your needs in five categories:

1. What do you need when you're in a **relationship** (of any kind) to feel **loved**?
2. What do you need in your job or **career** to feel **valued**?
3. What do you need in your **space** to feel **safe**?
4. What do you need in your **routine** to feel **whole** and **healthy**?

5. What do you need in your **spiritual** practice to feel **connected**?

Take the time to really explore these questions. Understanding what you need to feel loved, valued, safe, whole/healthy, and connected to your Higher Self is the only way you can get those needs met. Not only does this understanding give you a road map to meeting your own needs, it also gives others a road map to understanding you and meeting you where you are.

The same can be said for others in your life. Watching you outline your needs so clearly will help them do the same, so that you can understand how to meet their needs as well. This is mastery in relationships, making your communication and your connection with others feel more invigorating and fulfilling.

The most important part of this is that as you start to get clear on your needs, all those little ones inside you will feel fully seen. In being seen, they will learn to trust you, as your Higher Self, and let go of the projections that come through feelings like fear and anxiety. It's a win-win for all parts of you.

## REQUIREMENTS

Requirements stem from your needs. These are the conditions you have for others who get the opportunity to be in relationship with you. Being in relationship with you, especially as you embody your Higher Self, is a privilege. As a privilege, there is a cost to entry. It's not an open cattle call to anyone with a pulse. It's an exclusive invitation.

Do you see your time and energy that way? As an exclusive invitation? Or do you give it freely to whoever comes strolling by, expecting something from you?

This reframe is something your Higher Self sees as critical. If you are giving your energy freely, without return of energy, your life force is being siphoned away. Your Higher Self needs your life force so it can go to work making your dreams a reality. It is a precious resource, one that must be doled out carefully only to those who can meet it with equal energy and gratitude. This means there have to be some requirements.

I have a few requirements that help me ensure my relationships honor my Higher Self, that I don't have to hide her to win affection. Here are a few:

1. People need to be just as curious about me as I am about them. One-way conversations without a single question about me end after five minutes.

2. If you miss me, reach out to me; don't wait for me to reach out. Same goes for needing me; let me know what you need so I have the chance to give it to you. No silent expectations. They set us both up for failure.

3. Be accountable for your actions. If you feel you let me down, own it, and attempt to make a repair. It's what I will always do when I'm the one who's made the mistake, and I deserve the same in return.

To get clear on your requirements, spend a little time thinking and writing about the following:

1. If you knew that you'd be loved unconditionally, no matter what, what requirements would you have for people to win *your* love? What would they have to do?

2. Taking a look at your list of needs, bring to mind the most important people in your life today. What requirements do you have from them to help meet your needs?

3. Now, take some time writing about why these requirements are important. How will they change the way you show up in relationships? How will they enhance those relationships? How can they help the people in your life understand you better?

## CONSEQUENCES

Your needs and requirements are simply words if there are no consequences to not meeting them. Boundaries must be upheld to be actual boundaries. Consequences are there to ensure you get your needs met and don't continue to overlook bad behavior.

This one can be really hard for the people pleaser because that part of yourself believes love is scarce and you shouldn't do something that might make it go away. Let's remind that part of you that earned love by diminishing who you are and what you need isn't enduring because it's been gained through sacrifice. If someone loves us for a projection we put on, or because we shrink to some whiff of our full selves, it is not us they love.

If that people pleasing aspect really wants love, we need to show it that we are going to get that need met by getting it actual love, the real, enduring kind. The kind that won't blow away as you grow into your Higher Self and live your truth.

Your consequences don't have to be harsh or dramatic. They can be organic and commensurate with what's needed in the moment. Let's say for example that you need space to process your feelings when someone gives you direct feedback and that your requirement is that they put aside their need for instant gratification and give you that space. When that requirement is not met, what consequence would make the most sense to ensure your need is met?

It's not never speaking to the person again. That feels like a lot. What if instead the consequence is that you will go take the space, leave the room, end the conversation, and only come back to them when you have had the chance to process? The consequence in this example is as simple as meeting your own need instead of putting their needs in front of yours.

It's hard to preconceive consequences, so I won't make you try that in this moment. Instead, what I'd love for you to think about is how you can find the strength in the moment to lay down the consequence without fear. Or, better yet, do it even though you are experiencing the fear.

Consequences are just about creating space, upholding

your boundaries, so your needs can be met. That's going to be uncomfortable at first, but the work is about feeling that fear and doing it anyway. The more you do it, the more you'll notice that people don't go away that easily. The other person will actually end up feeling grateful for the opportunity to learn how to love you better.

And, if they don't, they weren't gonna stick around for the long run anyway. To those people we say, *See ya! Thanks for making space in my life for people who can meet me at my higher frequency.*

### Meeting at a Higher Frequency

The room you make through your boundaries creates space in your life for relationships where you, as your Higher Self, can be seen, celebrated, and rooted for. For every two people in your life that need you to remain small so they can be comfortable, there is another person you don't yet know who is just as interested in embodying their Higher Self as you are. They will jump at the chance to walk that journey alongside you.

Sure, that ratio means there will be fewer people to choose from, but what are you seeking in your relationships, quantity or quality? As your frequency elevates to that of your Higher Self, you'll start to more clearly see others who live at this new elevation. You'll just feel it. You'll sense it in the way they engage with you when you first meet or in the way you watch them live their own lives.

These are the people who will help you expand without pain or suffering, through inspiration and love. These people come along to show you what else is possible when you live in alignment with Higher Self, and they can come in all sorts of packages. They will show up in the form of lovers, friends, teachers, mentors, coaches, and more.

My life has been so full of these Higher Self souls over the past ten years that I feel deeply grateful every time I think about it. Of course, there's my husband, TJ, who sees me as my Higher Self and agreed in our wedding vows to always expand into his own Higher Self alongside me.

This isn't a one and done agreement either. Staying committed to this higher-frequency relationship takes work; there's maintenance. It's not a smooth path every day. Some days, as we figure out the complicated math of blending four kids who live in two different cities with two other co-parents and a hundred other obligations pulling at us, our tired, triggered, limited selves become more powerful than our Higher Self.

In those moments, we pick at each other, we become defensive with each other, and we sometimes disengage, leaving each other feeling misunderstood and isolated. We have a few rules that help us navigate these bumpier moments. First, we give each other space when we notice the other one is triggered. We don't make each other's triggered words and actions about ourselves. We give each other the grace to know it's not about the other person.

Second, we don't jump in to save each other by sacrificing our own truth to make the other feel better when we're triggered. We just simply take a step back and let the other have their process, remembering that in that triggering, there is a younger self that's looking for attention and healing. Our job, as partners, is to honor each other's younger selves' need for our attention. We do that by not making it about ourselves but by giving each other space to focus on this healing within.

Third, we go on dates. We make it a priority to find one night in the week, go somewhere outside of our day-to-day surroundings, and talk. Sometimes during these dates, we'll ask each other questions like *What do you need from me to feel more supported right now?* Or *What am I doing that might be making you feel less seen lately?*

We're brutally honest with each other during these conversations because we've also promised not to punish each other for our truth. Honesty is the only way to maintain the frequency of two Higher Selves coexisting and growing together. Saying the uncomfortable thing, the thing you have shame over feeling, out loud to your partner is how you stay at this frequency. As your partner allows this truth to exist without shame or retribution, you begin to notice how safe you are to be all versions of yourself with this human. Trust grows, and with it your connection grows even stronger.

Any time I feel like I'm hiding a truth inside, I know I'm choosing a lower frequency. I'm accountable to that choice. I ask myself, *Do you want a Higher Self relationship or not?* And usually I decide, as afraid as I may be to say the thing, that saying it is the only way to stay in a relationship as my Higher Self and allow TJ to do the same.

Outside of my relationship, I'm finding that as I continue to prioritize embodying my Higher Self, the people who love me and the new ones who come into my life also have permission to embody theirs. My family has shown me aspects of their Higher Self, modeling this expansion in all the ways I've shared with you and new ways every day.

My best friend, Melissa, who I've known for twenty years, is blossoming into the most confident, articulate, and self-actualized version of herself I've seen. We started a podcast together, only possible through both of our expansions, about the Higher Self, called *Signal*, and every week we sit and talk about a different roadblock or invitation to Higher Self and listening to our intuition.

I feel like I have to pinch myself that I get to work on a creative project like this with my best friend every week. I really don't know what to do with myself when people around the world actually tune in and send us heartfelt messages about how much our advice and our relationship is helping them to find their own truth and reach for more in their own relationships.

And then, there are the incredible new friends I'm meeting as I let my Higher Self lead the way. Spiritual teachers, neighbors, new friends that feel like old friends—all of whom I may have missed had I not worked so hard to embody my own Higher Self.

In my teaching of this work I've met incredible artists, authors, performers, and leaders—many of whom started as clients and became some of my most precious friends as they radiated their Higher Self in the world. Being around these people has created a reservoir in my life, a place I can go when I feel tapped and disconnected. A place where I can be reminded of what's possible when you live your truth without fear, a place of constant inspiration and the most dazzling dreams come true.

What about the people that can't get there? you may be asking yourself. I hear you. That's a real thing. Here's what I will tell you about those people: most of the ones you think may not be able to come along as you live at the frequency of Higher Self will be inspired and through that inspiration will wake up to their own truth, power, and inner wisdom. You can't force it. You can't drag them there. In fact, if you try, they will resent you and the process.

Forcing your way of living on others is, by the way, the fastest way to make them hate it enough to take the long route there. The only way is to model it, embody your Higher Self, and let them watch as you glide toward your dreams. It may not be totally smooth. They may reject you and your truth, but that's just their little limited belief selves. The more you show them what it's like not to align with fear but to embody truth, the more they will believe it is possible.

All they need is evidence—something to believe in. It's okay that their process doesn't look like yours. It may not be as quick or as tangible as your process, but it doesn't mean it is not happening within them. Will you have to let some people go so they can figure it out? Probably. I'm sorry if that scares you, but I want you to know, your love for yourself and for them is always a beacon that they can use to find their way back.

CHAPTER 14

# Emanating Love

Here you are, *at the* end of this journey.

Well, at the end of learning about this journey. Your pathway is still unfolding in many ways—and the real work begins as you go into the world and try living, daily, with your Higher Self. As you do, you will begin to witness a powerful new phenomenon I call the **flow**.

A flow state doesn't mean that everything becomes easy—believe me, I wish I knew the tricks for that!—but it means that your life has a new sense of *ease*. That confidence in who you are and what you deserve means that you'll no longer settle for things that don't amplify your joy or purpose. Before I let you go into your beautiful flow, guided by your Higher Self toward all that you desire and all that you're here to do, I want to tell you one last important thing: it gets to be easy now. That's what the flow stands for—*ease*.

Yes, you've strived in this life. You've kicked vigorously and splashed your arms around wildly as you've kept your head above water. You were resilient. You fought with every part of your being to stay alive. And you did it! You're here. You didn't drown. You worked hard to survive. BRAVO! I am so proud of you. Truly, what a wonder you are.

But it hasn't all been survival in your life, right? There have been moments of magic. Moments that took your breath away, that came when you least expected them, like a jolt. Those moments *flowed* to you.

Here's how that happened: Every once in a while, as you strove to navigate the rushing waters, you heard your Higher Self speak. With that gentle whisper, you remembered another way to swim in this river. You remembered that sometimes, you could just flip over, lie on your back, and let the current take you wherever you were meant to go.

In those moments, you experienced this phenomenon of flow, or moments that showed up with ease. These moments could only materialize because you stopped fighting and started listening to the deep reservoir of wisdom inside you. The fight had you married to fear, to the concept of survival alone, because the idea of thriving felt too far away.

But in those moments when you set down the fight and just let it happen, the flow reminded you that sometimes letting go is the path to arriving to your destination more whole, more ready to navigate life than ever before. In those moments you got a taste of what it's like to live in total alignment with Higher Self. And I want you to know, if it felt easy not to fight so hard, that's what being reconnected to your Higher Self is supposed to feel like.

The flow requires the trust and faith in Higher Self that we've talked about in these pages. It requires that you can access the knowing from deep within that you are being guided, gently, intentionally, toward the precise place you needed to be. That, my dear loves, gets to be easeful. It's okay for it to feel easy. The problem is that we often judge easy as not being "enough." If something feels easy, it's easy to imagine that we're being lazy or not trying as hard as we could. But that's not the case. Life won't always be easy, but you have everything you need now to experience ease in how you care for—and love—yourself.

I have faith that your Higher Self will remind you of this often as you tap in, but I wanted to make sure I reminded you, and all your precious little ones inside too, that hardness isn't the only path. Hard is simply something we've been taught to value and celebrate by a world filled with teachers and authority figures who have forgotten their own divinity. So, when it's easy, we believe somehow that it's not worthy, that *we* are not worthy. Remember, suffering is being disconnected from our Higher Self. So, let's reframe the concept of "hard" as what it is: disconnection.

Don't get me wrong, I'm not sitting here telling you that everything you want in life will just come to you with zero effort on your part. What I'm saying is that you *are* doing the work, and you have what you need to be connected to your intuition and purpose. Reawakening to your truth and living that truth, aka embodying Higher Self, is a feat. It requires so much constant inner dialogue, so much healing of little selves and limiting beliefs. This work requires so much accountability and presence, so much gratitude and trust, and so little judgment.

It also requires vision. Becoming clear on what you want, working with Higher Self to take one step, then the next toward that desire—that *is* you showing up and doing the work. You are engaged in the process. Your reward in doing all that work is the easefulness of the flow.

## Staying in Flow

While we've worked hard to bring awareness to all your conditioning, it will always be present. Your conditioning will try and tell you that the flow is not real, nor is Higher Self, and that if you want to succeed, you had better fight *hard*.

Just be aware, "hard" is a limiting belief instilled by others who are disconnected from their own Higher Self. Just because they haven't awoken to their inner wisdom, does that mean you need to stay asleep? Absolutely not. Awareness alone that this is just a limiting belief will help you put it into context when it pops up, demanding that you need to suffer to succeed.

Now that you've learned to see that conditioning as exactly what it is—a projection implanted by someone else's limitations—

when that feeling comes up inside you, you can identify it, love on it, and set it down. As you release that belief, you will make room for your Higher Self. To do that, you replace the limiting belief with the question: *What would my Higher Self do?*

Let's unpack that question a little more. If you were to embody the centered, rooted, dignified, and all-knowing perspective of your Higher Self, what would you do? When you ask that question, give yourself a pause and let the feeling come to you. The answer, let me remind you, is never far. Wait for that answer and move in the way it dictates.

The work is about getting that cynicism, judgment, shame, and all the rest of those limitations in check, lovingly.

Ask yourself now: *If I believed what I wanted was already flowing to me with ease, what would I do?*

Replace the information your limited selves are projecting with the answer to *that* question and see what begins to unfold for you.

I am reiterating this to you over and over, because if there's one thing I've learned from my own process, it's that even as a teacher of these truths, I find my own scared, limited selves can constantly throw me off course, filling my head with all the reasons it is not possible. When this happens, I spend a lot of time and energy on *why I can't or shouldn't do the thing*, which ultimately just slows me down. Believing these projections makes me resist where the flow is taking me, and instead takes me completely out of trust and faith.

Now, as someone who practices my own method, when that happens, I remind myself that those moments of limitation are just a sign that there's a younger version of me in there asking for some attention. So I give it to her. What I have learned to stop doing, though, is believing her projections.

I just let her have them and have learned to ask, in parallel, *If I believed what I wanted was already flowing to me with ease, what would I do?*

Instantaneously I hear my Higher Self answering that question.

Think of this interaction like an infinity symbol. It's a constant flow of conversation between your younger, more limited selves and your Higher Self. They are forever intertwined, forever in dialogue. This dialogue opens the flow.

As I remember how good it feels to be with Higher Self, how much less fighting and striving it requires, I'm able to unclench and surrender to the flow. This reminder that when I am reconnected to Higher Self, I get to operate from dignity instead of shame, possibility instead of limitation, and love instead of fear allows me to choose between fight or flow with clarity, and the choice is obvious.

### Everything Is Love

I met my brother—my sister's ex-husband—when I was thirteen. Up until that point, it had just been me, my mom, and my sister. Then my sister left home, moved to Philadelphia, and met Naheed. The first time I met Naheed, I decided he was my opposition—another guy taking her attention away from me—but Naheed had no interest in playing that role. He was too kind a person, too interested in what I thought and who I was; he grew on me very quickly.

By the time I was seventeen, Naheed and my sister were engaged and married by the end of that summer. Our family felt whole with Naheed in it. His presence felt like an obvious addition, making his not being a part of the family for the seventeen years prior feel like there had been a void in us somehow. He brought sunshine in. He made us laugh. He cared how we felt. He made himself a part of us.

In doing all of that, he also gave me something I didn't realize I had needed: a big brother. We'd bicker like brother and sister, laugh endlessly in front of the TV, and go to the movies, the mall, and McDonald's (still his favorite dining establishment). And yet, during that time, I knew that Naheed was an extension of my sister. I worried that his love for me was attached to his relationship with her. That he had to love me because he was married to her.

I was still unsure whether I was enough on my own for a brother like this.

You all remember how the rest of this story went. My sister came out shortly after their marriage, and they divorced when I was nineteen.

*This is it*, I'd tell myself. *You lose your big brother now.*

Truthfully, when I look back at my reactions to my sister's coming-out, I realize that so much of my anger toward her had to do with this fear of potential *loss*, of losing out on a family unit that I'd longed for and wanted to hold on to. But, somehow, through this life-changing event, my brother and I became even closer. We were there for each other, held each other in our sadness and confusion, used the same silliness we both embodied to bolster each other.

As life went on and he began to date again, I became sure he was lost to me. Who's gonna want their ex-sister-in-law around as they're trying to spark new romance? And yet still, my brother just went on being my brother, supporting me through my own divorce, showing up at every special occasion, birthday, holiday, event. Sitting in the waiting room with the rest of our family as I gave birth to both my kids. Fully diving into being their uncle, loving and spoiling them endlessly.

My brother was the one who told me it was time to move out of the house I shared with my ex-husband after we had separated and helped me buy a new place where the kids and I could start over again. He was the one who stood behind me, solid like an oak tree, pushing me to start my own business when I was a scared single mother. He was also the one who became ordained online and married TJ and me, tears stinging his eyes as he told the story of what I had meant to him, how I had been his life raft in so many ways.

Love was what made Naheed my brother. Not blood or relationships or circumstances. Just love. It is everything. It is the most binding force in nature. It *is* nature. Love is what makes us possible. We are here because of love. Love is what we come from, and it is all that we are. Everything is love, or is related to love, even fear. Fear is the absence of love. Hatred is fear manifest, which is the absence of love. Love is the material from which all is made.

"Are you telling me that a dictator is love?" you might be asking. "Or a killer, are they love?"

These are the natural questions that should come to mind when someone is telling you that everything is love. And to those questions I say again, yes. These people, at some point in their lives, had the material of love within them somewhere. Through neglect or abuse, that love became gnarled, and shriveled slowly into fear, which calcified into hate. Their "evil" is actually the decay of love.

Remember the flower that was left to rot on the kitchen counter? The one that was plucked up and either showered with love and attention or neglected and left to rot? That's what's happened to these people. They had the material of love, at some point, but it decayed because it was neglected. This doesn't mean we allow people to hurt us. Remembering that everything is love, even people who create harm, isn't an invitation to allow harm into our lives. Go back and read the chapter about boundaries if you need a reminder. You must protect your Higher Self. There must be lines drawn around you to allow for your expansion.

But remember, this life is not a story of OR, it is a story of AND. You can hold these boundaries personally AND expand your understanding of humanity. You can extend your view of humanity enough not to fall for the illusion of "us versus them." That's the transformation I'm asking us to lead right now. My hope is that in remembering our own divinity, our own Higher Self, we will remember that we are all connected, whether we agree with one another or not.

I told you the story of my brother because his story is one of a man who moved fully from his Higher Self, even in the face of pain. When you are in alignment with your Higher Self, you emanate love. This is the whole point, my loves. To remember that we are love and remember what love can do to heal us.

We need this healing desperately right now. We have lost ourselves. We've believed too fully in the illusion of our separateness. That illusion is killing us. Literally. We look at each other's differences and choose fear over love. And this is only possible when we are disconnected from our own divinity. Once we awaken to the truth, that we are our Higher Selves, not the fears that have been projected onto us, we have no choice but to emanate the love from which we come. It's just a natural part of the process.

Now, it is your responsibility to take the love coming from your Higher Self and push it outward into the world. This energy will have an impact. It is the counter-energy to all the fear and hate reverberating out there right now. In becoming your Higher Self, you are stepping into an important battle. Movies have taught us to think of it as the battle between good and evil. It's really a battle between fear and love, and I genuinely believe if we don't fight, we are on the precipice of losing it all.

This is your wake-up call. Now that you've reunited with your Higher Self, it's time to channel all that powerful love glowing from inside you and love all of us ferociously, so that others can watch you and learn to do the same. That is the only way we will survive.

Okay, whoa, no pressure, right?! I know, I just made an enormous ask. But not really. You already know what to do. It starts from within.

If you ever need a reminder, here are the six rules of your Higher Self to live by:

1. *Remember you are love, so love yourself fiercely first.*
2. *Trust your wisdom; it is a direct channel to your divinity.*
3. *Speak your truth loudly, so that you may stand tall in your dignity.*
4. *Don't judge yourself, and it will become impossible to judge others.*
5. *Embrace the parts of you that feel shame, so that will not seek to arouse shame in others.*
6. *Seek validation from within and it will become impossible to shun another.*

Live by these rules and you will approach everything with a deep, steady reservoir of love, and in doing that, you will have a ripple effect on everyone around you.

### The Ripple Effect

Let's go back to the purpose equation I shared with you in Chapter Six.

*The Purpose Equation: Natural Skills + the Experience of Joy or Fulfillment = Positive Impact on Others*

People mistake purpose as synonymous with career. It's not. Your purpose is what you're here to do as you experience life and your soul expands. This can mean that you create an impact on the world simply by the way you live, the love that emanates from you.

We mistake doing as our value; that's capitalism. Our value comes from being, radiating who we are, our Higher Selves, out into the world. Regardless of what your purpose is, your greatest purpose as an embodied soul is to radiate this love. This is all of our purpose, to emit this powerful energy, push it out into the world, and wrap each other in it.

As you embody your Higher Self and naturally emanate this love, you will notice tiny changes around you. You'll notice people change in your presence. In watching you elevate to a space of pure love, for yourself and for others, people around you will begin to desire that same vibration. Either this will set them on a path to their own awakening to Higher Self, or they will mimic what they see you doing.

Either way, your presence will multiply the presence of love exponentially. This is the ripple effect you will have when embodying your Higher Self. Imagine this ripple effect moving from your closest circle to your community, to your city, state, country. Take in just how powerful this ripple can be and know that you, yes, just you by yourself, can have a global impact by simply embodying your Higher Self as you move through the world.

My grandmother, Aziz Joon, was my first ripple. The way this woman loved was astonishing. She loved me from the moment she laid eyes on me because she saw something familiar. She saw, in me, the same power she had to transform heartache into healing through love.

Even though we lived on separate continents for most of her life, every time I was around my grandmother, I felt celebrated. She *saw* me, even when I acted out, rebelled, and pushed her love away. She was just always so proud, smiling as she'd take me in, a knowing twinkle behind her soulful eyes.

She died in Tehran when I was twenty-five. My mom took her back when the cancer started spreading across her body, knowing she'd want to be buried in the land that gave birth to her. On her deathbed, my mom laid next to her, holding her hand, and listening to her whisper her prayers.

The last thing she said was "God, take care of Mory."

I didn't know how to process that for a very long time, that my grandmother's last words were a prayer for me. But I understood it fully when I came into doing this work. My grandmother knew from the moment she laid eyes on me that my purpose was the same as hers: to heal through love. She felt our kinship and she believed in me.

Ripple.

My mother was the second ripple. Through all her heartbreak and disappointment, she loved me so fully, so fiercely that I genuinely never felt the absence of a second parent. There's a reason that my father is a footnote in this story; my mother made him one by wrapping me in such an intense amount of love, I never knew to miss him.

She did the same thing with joy. Even though I felt her sadness, my mother showed me that joy can coexist with deep heartbreak. We danced *so* much in my house growing up. My favorite story of my childhood is the time my mom and dad got into a huge fight and my dad stormed out of the house only to come back and find my mother, sister, and me dancing to my mom's favorite Persian song. That's how she rolls.

Love and joy buoyed my mother through her pain, and she built us a life raft from them. She implanted this love in me, this unending access to joy, and I, in turn, pass it on to my children, my family, my friends, my clients, and now, to you. My mother, and her mother before her, started this ripple of love for the world that emanates from within me. Actions they would have seen as small in the moment created a movement of love.

Ripple.

So many more ripples came to follow. I don't talk about my dad very much because I never really felt the loving ripple, but the Universe didn't leave me hanging there either. Instead, my uncle Mash, the very uncle we moved from Colorado to be near when my parents divorced, has become my dad in so many ways.

I feel like I got the experience of being loved by a father because of Uncle Mash. His devoted attention, his worrying about me, his exuberance over my successes, and his sadness over my heartbreaks—none of these things were a given. Uncle Mash didn't have to care as much as he did. He had a family of his own and his own stresses to overcome. Yet, he's rushed over every time we've needed him for the past forty-plus years. He has always just been there, heart wide open.

The day I left Maryland to head for California, my uncle Mash put the final box in the truck. He turned to me, pulled me into his big arms, and held me tight, crying with his whole heart, telling me how he never imagined the day would come when I lived across the country from him. Then, he let me go; despite his own breaking heart, he sent me off with genuine joy for what I was about to experience. Just like a dad.

*Ripple.*

## This Is Your Time

Now, my dear loves, it is your turn. Here's the thing: this is not the end, this is just your beginning. In fact, there is no end, really, ever. Life is about experience. Remember that soul inside? The one that needed tangible experiences from which to expand? Your life is being steered from that desire to experience life. That means there is no destination.

Your soul won't measure the quality of this embodied life by the destination you reached or how quickly you got there. The quality of your life will be measured by how you experienced it, and how much you expanded through that experience.

The goal is not to get anywhere, my loves. It's to live fully embodied in the truth, dignity, and wisdom of your Higher Self, through the highs and the lows. The goal of this life is to come back to who you are and navigate your life's experiences with your Higher Self in the driver's seat.

In this way you will experience life through a lens of love and joy instead of hardship and suffering. Living like this is contagious. Is there any greater impact you could have than this?

Stay with your Higher Self now. Make the commitment to put our Higher Self first. Promise to listen to your biggest desires. Take care of that scared little self inside. Say the truth out loud, even when you're scared. Choose to have faith in your inner world and let the path unfold without holding on so tightly to any one outcome.

Remember, it could be even greater than your greatest expectations. Trust that. Trust your desires, your longings, your values, and your truth. Follow those things like your life depends on it. Don't stop for anyone. They will be okay. They will grow because you are making this commitment to embody your Higher Self. You will be emanating love from this new frequency. Remember that.

You were born whole. You lacked nothing. You came into this world aligned to Higher Self, and you've worked your way back into this alignment through a lot of pain, confusion, and suffering. In this reunion, you've been reawakened to the truth that you are not alone, not only because your Higher Self is always guiding you, but because you now remember that you are connected to every other living soul.

There is no connection to Higher Self without connection to the rest of the universe. We are all a part of that interlacing web, and your Higher Self will always remind you that you are an integral part of something much, much greater.

Now, take a big, deep, beautiful breath, sit up tall, feel that pulsing power of your Higher Self within. Go out into the world, head held high, whole, purposeful, and powerful, and make us better. We need you. We need all your power, all your love, all of you.

Go show them who you are.

Go show them your Higher Self.

# Acknowledgments

*They say it takes a village,* but in my case, to write this book, it took several. Without them, none of these words would have made it on this page. I am going to attempt to name and thank them all. The first is my family. My beautiful mom, Mahin, my sister, Mojgan, and my brother, Naheed, the nucleus of my cell, have believed in this book and my ability to write it unwaveringly from day one. My cousin, but actually baby sister, Anais, who stands by me and helps me really articulate my thoughts and my gifts through countless brainstorms, never giving up on me, even when I beg her to. Her father, my uncle Mash (my bonus dad), and my aunt Carlene, and my cousin Ashkon and his wife, Marcia, have been a consistent source of love and laughter for me always. My other bonus dad, Al, my mom's husband, takes such deep interest in my work, asking me question after question, pushing me to keep clarifying what I do and how I do it. My incredible nephew Arman, who is an inspiration of a human being. His gentle soul, thoughtful nature, and dedicated fight for justice and integrity have become my compass in so many ways. My nephew Daniel, for being my "sisto," no matter who disagrees, and Anushree, for always showing up for me. My sister-in-law, Mashael, who just gets me, reminds me I don't have to work so hard to be seen and understood. My mother-in-law, Kayse (Nana), for her excitement about this book and asking me about it every time she saw me until her last breath, and my brother-in-law, Todd, who made every second I spent with him feel exciting and full of wonder, right up until his passing. My father-in-law, Tom, who, as a retired Olympic ski coach, always reminds me that coaching others is about seeing their greatest selves and reflecting it back to them. And, my own father, whose belief in himself and desire for the genuine well-being of his family drove him, with courage, to leave his home and make a life here in the United States, which gave me the freedom to write these very words. Thank you from the bottom of my heart to each and every one of you. Without you, there would be no me.

Then there is the family I have built. Reina, my fierce and beautiful girl; Kian, my "sonshine" who radiates light into my life; Keegan, the most loving man you'll ever meet; Quinn, the sweet and silent reminder that life is full of little joys; and my incredible, supportive, strong, gentle, deeply intuitive, and remarkable husband, TJ. Thank you all for listening to hours and hours of me "yapping," as you like to say, about intuition. Thank you for supporting me even when it took me away from you. Thank you for believing in me enough to tell me to keep going, even when I was exhausted and ready to give up and hang out with you guys instead. I adore you.

To the village that is made up of incredible friends, I can't believe you guys were right—I can write a book! This village spans the globe, but I want to focus on two tribes. To my East Coast village, beginning with my best friend, Melissa; to Rhea and Alok, who quite literally reminded me who I was; to my community of strong, beautiful, and deeply insightful humans in Maryland: Lea, Rami, Aaryn, Rebecca, Christy, Suzanne, and Chinyere. You all carried me here by loving me and my kids and reminding me that being a single mom meant absolutely nothing. That I always had a place with you and that I could achieve anything. Thank you. My West Coast village, who came together so quickly and so meaningfully, the minute I put the signal out. Jen, Sarah, Dustin, Jennifer, Rendy, Stacie, Nakisa, Tommy, Alex, Cyrus, Dylan, Chrissy, Kane, Andrew, and Katja, your love made relocating to California while trying to write a book so much less isolating and so much more fun. Thank you.

My literary village. My brilliant agent, Lauren Hall, who received a very different book proposal from me and looked me dead in the eye and said, "Will you please just write a book about intuition?" Kelsey Grode, my amazing collaborator, talked to me for hours, helping me organize the volumes of things I wanted to say, then spending painstaking hours reading my words and offering so much insight and encouragement to this first-time author. And Anna Montague at Harper Collins, who believed in me and this work enough to take a chance on me. Thank you all for helping me take all that I am and put it into this book. You've given me an enormous gift.

To my guides and ancestors, thank you for your unconditional love and sacrifice so that I may represent all your hopes, wishes, struggles, and triumphs in my quest to help you, me, and the world heal. And finally, to my Higher Self: you were right, you always are. Thank you for never leading me astray.

# Notes

Chapter 1: You Are Divine

1. Samantha Taylor-Colls, R.M. Pasco Fearon, "The Effects of Parental Behavior on Infants' Neural Processing of Emotion Expressions," *Child Development*, Volume 86, Issue 3, May/June 2015, Pages 877–88, https://srcd.onlinelibrary.wiley.com/doi/10.1111/cdev.12348.

Chapter 5: The World Around You

1. Walker, Alice, "David Icke: The People's Voice," Alice Walker: The Official Website, July 19, 2013, https://alicewalkersgarden.com/2013/07/david-icke-we-are-change/.
2. Gerald J. Prokopowicz, *The Reform Era and Eastern U.S. Development, 1815–1850 (American Eras, 5)*, Gale Research Inc., 1998.
3. Ken Robinson, "Do schools kill creativity?" TED2006, February 2006, https://www.ted.com/talks/sir_ken_robinson_do_schools_kill_creativity?language=en.
4. Giorgio Parisi, "Nobel Prize–winning physicist explains the power of intuition in scientific discovery," *BIGTHINK*, July 2023, https://bigthink.com/thinking/power-intuition-science/.
5. Elizabeth Appell, "Anais Nin and I are in lockstep," July 24, 2018, https://readelizabeth.com/2012/12/anais-nin-and-i-are-in-lock-step/.

## Chapter 10: Learning the Language of Your Soul

1. Cathy Malciodi, "The Body Holds the Healing," *Psychology Today*, December, 29, 2022, https://www.psychologytoday.com/us/blog/arts-and-health/202212/the-body-holds-the-healing#:~:text=Trauma%20and%20the%20Disembodied%20Self,and%20their%20internal%20felt%20sense.